A Treasury of Business Humor

Edited by
James E. Myers

THE LINCOLN-HERNDON PRESS, INC.
818 South Dirksen Parkway
Springfield, Illinois 62703

A Treasury of Business Humor

Published by

The Lincoln-Herndon Press, Inc.
818 S. Dirksen Parkway
Springfield, Illinois 62703
(217)   522-2732

Printed in the United States of America

LIBRARY OF CONGRESS CATALOGUING-IN-PUBLICATION DATA

ISBN 0-942936-28-0 $12.95
Library of Congress Catalogue Card Number 96-77610
First Printing

Typography by

Spiro Affordable Graphic Services
Springfield, Illinois

TABLE OF CONTENTS

INTRODUCTION

America IS business in the sense that most Americans make their living and their contribution to our society working in business. We are a superb business people, paying our workers good wages, offering our customers outstanding products, willing to compete with the business of other nations (often when at a disadvantage to ourselves because of wage differentials).

In other words, we are a supremely confidant, hard-working, imaginative and thorough people devoted to making our individual business America's business...and doing it successfully.

In pursuing our various courses of business, tensions often develop, feelings become raw and sensitive and the spirit droops. That marks the spot where laughter, humor, the telling joke, the hilarious illustrative cartoon enter the American business picture, helping to ease feelings, illustrate important data and relax tense circumstances. Therefore, humor is essential to the fun, romance, success and durability of those engaged in American business.

Everybody knows that laughter is good for the body's mental and physical health (it's "the best medicine"). It's also a known fact that humor–at the appropriate time and setting–is good for business whether in administration, buying, selling, advertising or manufacturing an American product.

In this book's collection, the reader will find jokes, one-liners, cartoons, poems, that illustrate the statements above. You do not have to be a "businessperson" (remember when it used to be "businessman"?) to enjoy the humor, but the actual businessperson will find the hilarious contents a genuine contribution to personal life and health (remember..."laughter is the best medicine") as well as to the fun and efficiency needed in business.

The expressed human need for laughter goes back to biblical times: "A joyful heart is good medicine but a broken spirit dries up the bones." Proverbs 17:22

On a more recent count, Norman Cousins says: "Laughter is a form of jogging for the innards."

Or, consider this evaluation of the fate of the sour soul: "A person without a sense of humor is like a wagon without springs - jolted by every pebble in the road."

And Mohammed, in his Koran states: "He deserves paradise who makes his companions laugh."

With all this wisdom telling us to laugh, to enjoy the humorous side of life, well, we'd best take it to heart and say:

ENJOY (and that's an order from the boss!)

1
EXECUTIVES, BOSSES, and HEAD HONCHOS

"If all executives were laid end to end, they would not reach a conclusion."
Attributed to George Bernard Shaw

✳ ✳ ✳ ✳ ✳

In the business world, the executive must know something about everything, his staff must know everything about something, and the switchboard operator knows everything.

✳ ✳ ✳ ✳ ✳

My boss was a workaholic, endangering his health, until a friend one day said, "George, what in the hell do you want. . . the world is nothing to a man when his wife is a widow."

✳ ✳ ✳ ✳ ✳

At a recent Board of Directors meeting, a member of the board got into a heavy argument with the president, who said, "I may not agree with what you think, Sir, but I'll defend to the death your right to shut up!"

✳ ✳ ✳ ✳ ✳

A dandy way to make money is the old-fashioned way of inheriting it!

✳ ✳ ✳ ✳ ✳

Our vice-president is a woman and a fancy-pants. She's so toney that she won't eat lady fingers unless they're manicured!

✳ ✳ ✳ ✳ ✳

My boss ought to spell his name backwards. It'd be more appropriate to spell it S.S.O.B. (forget that first S!)

What can you say about our vice-president that hasn't already been said about pimples!

✳ ✳ ✳ ✳ ✳

Show business can be a trying profession. Last year, a Broadway producer was producing a radically different show. . . a moral, inspirational musical comedy, but he demanded that all female participants be virgins. Accordingly, one girl went to her physician and got a statement that she was a virgin. Next day she took the statement to the producer, who looked at it and then exploded: "What the hell good is this. . . it's dated yesterday!"

✳ ✳ ✳ ✳ ✳

There's nothing to winning, really. That is, if you happen to be blessed with a keen eye, an agile mind and no scruples whatsoever.
Alfred Hitchcock

✳ ✳ ✳ ✳ ✳

I wish my boss would quit using hair oil. The last time he went to his barber, the guy asked him if he wanted an oil change.

✳ ✳ ✳ ✳ ✳

The executive rushed into the country club dressing room just in time. "I almost didn't make it," he said to the three fellows waiting for him to complete their foursome. "The work piled into the office and I almost stayed there. It was a toss-up whether I'd work or play golf with you. On the fifteenth toss, you won."

✳ ✳ ✳ ✳ ✳

Are you bothered by constant charitable requests? Here's good advice from Mark Twain on how to handle the situation. "When you are fired by an eager impulse to contribute to charity, wait and count to forty; to save three-quarters, wait and count to sixty. To save it all, count to sixty-five."

"Businesses should live within their income," as Josh Billings said, "even if they have to borrow money to do it."

✳ ✳ ✳ ✳ ✳

To be successful: RISE EARLY. . .WORK LATE. . .STRIKE OIL!
        Paul Getty

✳ ✳ ✳ ✳ ✳

Oil, mostly Middle East oil, moves the world. The industry developed this joke to describe the origins of the business. It seems that God told Moses just how he would divide the land of the Middle East between the Arabs and the Jews. Moses listened carefully, then repeated God's words to be sure he'd heard accurately.

"Dear God," Moses said, "if I understood you correctly, you are giving the oil to the Arabs and we get to cut off the tips of our WHAT!"

"I INTEND TO ACQUIRE YOUR STAND IN EITHER A LEVERAGED BUYOUT OR A HOSTILE TAKEOVER."

By working faithfully eight hours a day, you may eventually get to be a boss and work twelve hours a day.
Robert Frost

* * * * *

My rise to the top was through sheer ability and inheritance.
Malcolm Forbes

* * * * *

Murray Campton had made it big, really big, in the department store business. A reporter from his hometown was interviewing him and asked what was the most important personal characteristic that had led to his success.

"It's will power, that's the reason, the main reason for my success."

"Could you explain that for me?" the reporter asked.

"Sure," the big shot said. "My father died and in his will left the entire chain of department stores to me!"

* * * * *

"A tragedy has happened to me, of all people," the small manufacturer said to his friend. "My plant burned down and now everything is gone."

"Do you have a testimonial as to the cause and all of the fire," his friend asked, "so you can collect insurance?"

"I sure did. But that, too, was lost in the fire."

* * * * *

There was this guy who owned a large but unsuccessful men's suit manufacturing business. He had over fifty suits pending!

* * * * *

Everybody who worked under Phineal P. Walker, president of his self-owned company, detested him for the conceited ass he was.

One day, a junior officer came into the president's office and told his secretary that, after lunch, he had seen the boss at the nearby cathedral deep in prayer.

"Prayer?" replied the secretary. "To whom?"

If that arrogant, conceited vice-president of our company would swallow his pride, he'd gain thirty pounds.

* * * * *

The president of the corporation, addressing the annual Board of Directors meeting, said, "Ladies and gentlemen, I have doubled last year's volume, tripled our profit, and the dividend forthcoming will be quadrupled."

The Chairman of the Board stood and said, "Thank God for you, Sir. We think YOU ARE GOD!"

"I know! I know!" said the president. "And it's such an awful responsibility!"

* * * * *

My boss is almost entirely bald-headed. When people remark about it, he says, "Well, my folks always said that I'd come out on top!"

* * * * *

You can be sure it'll be a bad day when your birthday cake collapses under the weight of the candles.

* * * * *

You know it's going to be a bad day when you turn on the news and they show emergency routes from the city.

* * * * *

A conference is a gathering of important people who singly can do nothing but collectively can decide that nothing can be done.
Fred Allen

* * * * *

The president of our company is an utterly conceited ass. I was told that when he checked out of a hotel in Manhattan, the mirror in his room was still warm a week later!

Whenever you are sitting across from some important person, always picture him sitting there in a suit of long underwear. That's the way I always operated in business.
Joseph Kennedy

* * * * *

It's hard to figure some bosses. Mine just called me into his office, saying, "Now, I'm about to mix fun with business. You're fired!"

* * * * *

Did you hear about the executive who gave his secretary a very large present, because she was late. . .two months late.

* * * * *

A priest and the president of a major manufacturing company died, and both appeared at the Pearly Gates at the same time. The priest was given the key to a tiny room, but the corporation president was shown to a mansion. The priest was upset, saying, "How is it that I, a sinless priest, am given this small room while this 'go-get em' president of a huge corporation gets the elegant treatment?"
"Well, you see," St. Peter explained, "we never had a president of a major American corporation here before."

* * * * *

The boss's wife complained that her husband never bought her a present for their anniversary and that this year she'd like him to give her something to drive. So he bought her a sledge hammer and a chisel!

* * * * *

Today there's a new definition for a housekeeper, especially for our boss who is on his third wife. His two previous wives were housekeepers. . .they got to keep the house!

* * * * * *

The boss called in one of his assistants and said, "I've been told that you went to church and prayed for a raise. How dare you go over my head!"

An office supply company just advertised a new conference table that sleeps twenty.

✻ ✻ ✻ ✻ ✻

All work and no play makes jack. . ..

✻ ✻ ✻ ✻ ✻

The difference between the right word and the nearly right word is the difference between lightning and the lightning bug.

Mark Twain

✻ ✻ ✻ ✻ ✻

The president of our company is a really rich man. Why, when he goes to enter an airplane, his wallet is considered carry-on luggage.

DAVE Bonerten

"Wilson, you're definitely middle management material."

Talk about ostentatious! Our neighbor, president of his company, is that and more. He put out a bird cage with. . .a salad bar!

✻ ✻ ✻ ✻ ✻

My boss is really unselfish, the kind of boss who always shares the credit with the one who does the work.

✻ ✻ ✻ ✻ ✻

The executive was explaining his success and started out by saying: "I didn't have a cent when I started out in this business."
"Well, how did you get started?" he was asked.
"I wired home for money," he said.

✻ ✻ ✻ ✻ ✻

Two executives were discussing men's fashion. One of them said, "I don't pay a lot of attention to fashionable dress. Not any more, not since I bought an expensive silk suit with two pair of paints, then burned a hole in the jacket."

✻ ✻ ✻ ✻ ✻

They still have southern planters in Alabama. This one guy was an undertaker in Selma and his son was also successful, having over a thousand people under him. He was the caretaker in the Selma, Alabama, cemetery.

✻ ✻ ✻ ✻ ✻

GLOSSARY OF GOBBLEDYGOOK

The Gobbledygook	A Reasonable Facsimile of The Meaning	Source (The person who suggested the gobbledygook to us or who enthusiastically likes or dislikes the particular term; or uses it in every other breath of their own conversation-we ain't saying for which reason)

With some allowance for errors in translation

A program	Any assignment that can't be completed by one telephone call.	Ford Bond
Channels	The trail left by an inter-office memorandum.	Dorothy Dean

Status Quo	This mess we're in.	Ruth Taylor
To expedite	To confound confusion with commotion.	Harry Neafie
Expediter	One who does the same while riding fast trains and staying in good hotels.	Bill McGaughey
Efficiency expert	A guy who trains expediters.	Howard Tickle
Coordinator	A guy who has a desk between two expediters.	Bill Haworth
Liaison officer	A person who talks well and listens better but has no authority to make a definite statement.	Clifton Web
Consultant	An ordinary guy a long way from home.	C. W. Green
Criteria	Measures which the other guy uses to underestimate what you have already overestimated the deal to be worth.	Henry Turnbull
Incentive Program	A scheme to titillate a submerged urge.	Anderson & Brant, Inc.
To activate	To make carbons and add more names to the memorandum.	Joseph Basine
To implement a program	To hire more people and open more field offices.	Dick Testut
Under consideration	Never heard of it.	Bob Howard
Under active consideration	We're looking in the files for it.	Cy Perkins
In transmittal	We're sending it to you because we're tired of holding the bag.	Rosser Reeves
F. Y. I.	Found Yesterday, Interested?	Michael Carr
Across the board	I'll back up everything you say if you'll front for me.	A. Boyd Zook
A meeting	A mass mulling of master minds.	John Martin
A conference	A place where conversation is substituted for the dreariness of labor and the loneliness of thought.	Hubbell Robinson
In conference	He's gone out.	Dr. A. A. Hutschnecker
Can't be disturbed	Nobody knows where.	John Sloan
Out of the city	He hopes nobody will find out.	W. R. Parrott
Liaison	The longest distance between points of view.	Alice Hughes
To negotiate	To seek a meeting of the minds without a knocking together of heads.	Fredrick H. Groel
Orientation	Getting used to being a $1-year man.	A. B.. Lichtenstein
Re-orientation	Getting used to working again.	Austin Fisher
Retread expert	One who should be retired.	Gurney Williams
Reliable source	The guy you met just before going to press.	Frank LaClave
Informed source	The guy who told the guy you met.	Max Cook
Unimpeachable source	The guy who wrote the rumor down originally.	Turnley Walker
A contact	A source through which rumors can be had at wholesale.	Charles W. Ferguson
To be on the inside	To be able to get fresh rumors even below wholesale.	Abel Green

Term	Definition	Attribution
Inside dope	Anything a dope on the outside will believe.	Les Hafner
A clarification	To fill in the background so detailed that the foreground must go underground.	Arthur Motley
A modification of policy	A complete reversal which nobody admits.	Raymond Walsh
To spell out	To break big hunks of gobbledygook down into little hunks of gobbledygook.	Tony Hutson
Rationale	Highbrow version of "to spell out."	Toni Kassebohm
To break down by categories	To put in separate piles.	Lloyd Shaffer
Conservation	Something everybody is in favor of having everybody else do so there will be enough of whatever it is that's being conserved to supply the guy who can get it for you wholesale.	Ely Culbertson
A synthesis	A compounding of detailed bewilderment into a vast and comfortable confusion which offends no one.	Chen Ah-Moa
Back to the grass roots	A cry uttered periodically by both bureaucrats and businessmen to temper their complete detachment from life.	C. Scott Fletcher
Per diem	Sub-subsistence for a GI traveling man.	Robert Lenhart
Ad Lib	Free wheeling conversation.	Mary Bass
Ad Hoc	We don't know either, but it has nothing to do with a pawn shop.	Richard Rossheim
To wit	A misprint which appears frequently in legal gobbledygook.	T. Bagg, LL.D.
Frame of reference	The word border around a nebulous analysis.	Henry Kite
Will advise in due course	If we ever figure it out, we'll let you know.	Ernest Fender
A wafflebottom	A guy who has been waiting in a lobby equipped with canebottom chairs.	Jerry Klutz
Held in abeyance	A state of race for a disgraceful state.	Donald Beddoe
To give someone the picture	A long confused and inaccurate statement to a newcomer.	William Ramsey
Problem area	Same boundaries as the District of Columbia.	Florence Schwartz
In due course	Never.	Mary Margaret McBride
With reference to	This letter has to begin somewhere.	Richard Kollmar
An open mind	Exactly that.	P.D. Fahnestock
To mastermind	To avoid blame for not doing while getting credit for the doing of others.	Ben Gross
An overall statement	One that's over everybody's head.	Arthur Faught
Quota	Half as much as you need when you can't get all you want.*	Lawrence Landsman

*Such as paper to publish a best seller like *The Care and Feeding of Executives.*

Government board	Long, narrow and wooden.	H.D. Thompson
Research work	Hunting for the guy who moved the files.	Petie Schwartz

10

Formula (for success)	Knowing the ropes well enough to pull the right strings.	Connie Bannister
Point up the issue	Expand one page to 15 pages.	Allan Wilson
Functional control	You tell him what to do and he'll tell you where to go.	Ken Beirn
To needle	To administer an administrative goose.	T. S. Repplier
To sparkplug	To administer an administrative hotfoot.	Donald Hammond
To spearhead	To shove in and break off.	Philip Furhrmann
Topside authorities	The guys on the first row of the organizational chart.	Lt. Wm. B. Horstman
Circular file	Wastebasket. Large ones make for cleaner desks.	Samuel Slotkin
Carbon paper	A thin flexible substance, the invention of which has multiplied the scope of the executive and bureaucratic world many fold.	Mark Hanna
Mimeograph	A mechanical device, the invention of which has even outdone the proliferating effects of carbon paper.	Reidar Torsen
IBM machines	It'll Be Murder (when executives fully realize their proliferating potentialities).	Sylvia Porter
Briefcase	A cowhide satchel full of itinerant pigeonholes.	Connie Ernst
Procedure	Everyday routine rigmarole.	Ed Gottlieb
Protocol	Full dress patent leather rigmarole.	Paul Garrigue
Preliminary draft	A directive issued quickly before Congress repeals the act.	Mike Rowell
Congressional record	A "Dear Diary" for solons.	Tom Lamb
Federal register	A "Damned Diary" for businessmen.	Thomas Spain
The OWI	The Paragraph Troops of the Chairborne Infantry.	George R. Evans
A directive	A government order of uncertain intent issued on unreliable authority.	Herman Hettinger
A docket	The recipe for a directive.	Ken Ellington
Letter of transmittal	A way to pass the buck.	Grafton Lee Brown
A survey is being made on this	We need more time to think of an answer.	Robert J. Powderly
Further substantiating data necessary	We've lost your stuff. Send it again.	Edgar Williamson, Jr.
Vice President	The guy who does the work for which the President gets the credit.	Nick Kenny
To explore the ramifications	And brother just wait 'til you see what we think of.	Jim McGoodwin
Confidential memorandum	There wasn't much time to mimeograph this.	Cameron Day
Top secret	We may be wrong about this so don't circulate it.	Col. Tom. H.A. Lewis
A conference	A meeting of Executives to listen while the boss talks on long distance.	Bruce Robertson
Radio critic	Anybody who spent a week in the hospital listening to the radio.	George Rosen

Sponsor	A manufacturer who thinks he's David Belasco.	John Crosby
Company policy	Excuse for unpleasantness.	Dr. Gus Landau
Career girl	A woman who comes to New York to make her fortune, or somebody.	Earl Wilson
Contract	An obeisance to legality.	Dr. Arnold J. Zurcher
Note and initial	Let's spread the responsibility for this.	Capt. Tim Healy
Exclusive news item	None of the other columnists would print this one.	Danton Walker
Press conference	A personal encounter with reporters where more questions are asked than answered.	Sid Weiss

The Care and Feeding of Executives
by Millard C. Faught & Laurence Hammond
Wormwood Press. New York   1945

❊ ❊ ❊ ❊ ❊

If two men can dig a ditch in seven hours and two other men can dig the same size ditch in three hours, why did the first two quit and come to work in my office?

❊ ❊ ❊ ❊ ❊

The boss fired this one employee and his secretary asked, "When do you plan on filling the vacancy?"
The boss replied, "He didn't leave any."

❊ ❊ ❊ ❊ ❊

The key speaker at the convention was a bore, and he went on and on until the audience was frantic. At last, after two hours, he stopped, saying, "I apologize for speaking so long. But I lost my watch, you see, and didn't. . ." A voice from the audience interrupted him: "Look behind you. . .there's a calendar on the wall."

❊ ❊ ❊ ❊ ❊

The main occupational hazard of top executives is burnout. Lower caste executives have a different problem. It's mildew.

"BAD NEWS. . .OUR COMPUTER HAS BEEN TAKEN CONTROL OF BY SOME 12 YEAR-OLD IN ALBANY!"

He was the messiest executive we'd ever had. They had to build a retainer wall next to his desk. And they forced him to take out liability insurance just in case!

✳ ✳ ✳ ✳ ✳

The suggestion box in our office is wide and wrinkled with a huge bottom. It reminds us of our boss.

✳ ✳ ✳ ✳ ✳

You ask what's the difference between golf and bowling? For one thing, it's almost impossible to lose a bowling ball!

Coffee is as much a part of the office as stamps, paper clips, rubber bands, and scotch tape. . .and tastes about the same.

✳ ✳ ✳ ✳ ✳

An executive told this story to illustrate the need to always take advantage of a decent, necessary opportunity when it is offered.

A man was stranded on the desert and crawled along, finally coming to a tent. He called out, "Help me, I need water."

"Ain't got no water," a voice called back. "But I got a necktie for you."

"I need only water," the man moaned. "No thanks." And the man crawled on, soon coming to another Bedouin tent. "Water, water," he called. "I need water."

Again the same reply: "Ain't got no water. But I got a shirt for you."

"No. . .no shirt. I need water."

The poor, lost soul crawls on and finally comes to an oasis but there's a guard at the gate. "Please let me in," he begs of the guard.

The guard shakes his head, saying: "You can't come in, Sir, you have got to have a shirt and tie to enter!"

✳ ✳ ✳ ✳ ✳

In these huge corporations, the lower executives have to push the elevator's "up" button to get to the parking garage.

✳ ✳ ✳ ✳ ✳

TEDIOUS TRACT
Shareholders must
Be kept informed
Of company actions
That affect us.
But, pray tell, has
A holder anywhere
Actually read a
Corporate prospectus?
             Charles Upton
             Pepper & Salt
             Wall Street Journal - April 7, 1996

The one thing I like about my boss's egotism is that he never talks about other people, only himself!

✳ ✳ ✳ ✳ ✳

The American Civil War was going badly, chiefly because General George Brinton McClellan refused to fight even though his army was superior in numbers and training. President Abraham Lincoln was fed up with McClellan's do-nothing leadership and wrote him a letter that said: "General McClellan, if you don't plan to use the army, I should like to borrow it for a while."
Yours respectfully, A. Lincoln

✳ ✳ ✳ ✳ ✳

Did you hear about the company that was having cash-flow problems? It finally solved the trouble by adding antifreeze to the flow.

✳ ✳ ✳ ✳ ✳

Jonas C. Clemens, head of a major U.S. corporation, once said: "I'll never understand why the Women's Lib movement hasn't mentioned the male chauvinism in calling our mail room, just that! I guess it's because to change it to 'Person Room' would free it to be called, rather, 'Poison Room.'"

✳ ✳ ✳ ✳ ✳

Our treasurer is a true tightwad. He's got short arms and low pockets.

✳ ✳ ✳ ✳ ✳

The harassed office manager called the Suicide Prevention League and got an answering machine that said, "Please leave your name and number and the bridge from which you are now considering jumping."

✳ ✳ ✳ ✳ ✳

Few lower executives get the big-head. Why? Well, in their small offices, a big head wouldn't fit.

It is said that today's office furniture was designed by asses but certainly not *for* them.

✳ ✳ ✳ ✳ ✳

The president of his company retired at seventy and found life kind of dull. So one night, he decided to go to a dance at the senior citizens center, where he found a most attractive woman of his vintage.

While they danced, he told her he was a widower, the retired president of a large manufacturing company in which he owned a large amount of stock that, along with his nice pension, made him quite comfortable.

His dancing partner said, "You know what? You remind me of my third husband."

"My goodness! How many husbands have you had?"

"Two."

✳ ✳ ✳ ✳ ✳

The difference between a salary and income? Well, salary is what you get for the hard work you do. Income is what you get for the hard work your father did.

✳ ✳ ✳ ✳ ✳

My boss is really stingy. Just to get a legal pad from him, you have to pass the bar exam.

✳ ✳ ✳ ✳ ✳

Albert Einstein, the great physicist, had advertised for laboratory help. The first to appear for interviews said, "Sir, my name is Robert George. I have an IQ of 140."

"That's fine," said the professor. "You and I can surely discuss my theory of relativity."

The next man came in and said, "My name is Oliver Wentz and I have an IQ of 165."

"Wonderful," said Einstein, "we'll be able to discuss the theory of physics."

The next man in said, "My name is Bertrum Pisgard and I have an IQ of 110."

"That's just fine," said Einstein, "because you and I can discuss which stocks I should buy."

16

My boss is the stingiest man in the city. He requires all memorandums to be done on a single sheet of paper. Why? He's saving on paper clips!

✻ ✻ ✻ ✻ ✻

A fellow has been having headaches and goes to his doctor who tells him, "Your brain has a serious disease."

"Oh, golly," the poor guy says. "Just what can you and I do about that?"

"Well, there is the possibility of a brain transplant but. . .the problem with that is cost. It's not covered by medical insurance."

"Don't let that worry you, Doctor. I have money. What'll it cost me?"

"That depends on the kind of brain you want. A secretary's brain costs about $40,000. But an accountant's brain costs near to $55,000, while an executive's brain will run half a million."

"Wow! Half a million! How do you explain the difference between the $40,000 and $500,000, Doctor?"

"Well, as you know, an executive's brain hardly gets used!"

✻ ✻ ✻ ✻ ✻

Our boss is so cheap. . .he sits in a restaurant with his back to the check. And if that doesn't work, he pleads a 'reach' impediment!

✻ ✻ ✻ ✻ ✻

Boss: "Sit down, John, while I tell you about the salary increase I planned for you."

"Oh boy, that's great, Sir. When does it become effective?"

"Just as soon as you do!"

✻ ✻ ✻ ✻ ✻

Never speak at a business meeting unless you have to. Why? Because it is better to remain silent and be thought of as a fool, than to speak and remove all doubt of it.

"WE'VE BEEN USING A LOT OF TEMPS LATELY."

✳ ✳ ✳ ✳ ✳

Some months after the boss had talked to his employee about that pay increase becoming effective when he did, the boss called him into the office once again and handed him his pay envelope, saying: "You'll find something extra in your pay envelope this week, John."
"Gee, that's great. What is it?"
"A pink slip!"

✳ ✳ ✳ ✳ ✳

Modern business leaves no stone unturned to get the job done, as illustrated in my office where DIAL-A-PRAYER also has a fax number!

✳ ✳ ✳ ✳ ✳

Toot your own horn enough and people will stay out of your way.

Harry Smith owned a small department store back in the fifties. And he was known as the cheapest-chinsiest employer in town. Well, when he passed away all the employees went to the funeral. One of them noticed that there were only four pallbearers. He asked the funeral director why that was.

"Well," replied the director, "it was the strangest thing. We started out with six, but then Old Man Smith sat up in his casket and let the other two go!"

※ ※ ※ ※ ※

What a Weigh to Go (for overweight executives)

The Wabash County Hospital, Columbus, OH, is circulating a list of "Sure Calorie Burners" from the New Direction Weight Control System:

> Jumping to conclusions–87
> Pushing your luck–103
> Running around in circles–187
> Tooting one's own horn–52
> Beating your head against the wall–221
> Making mountains out of molehills–179
> Swallowing your pride–148
> Jumping on the bandwagon–36
> Fishing for compliments–29
> Bending over backward–126

> Reprinted with permission of Marcia Proffitt
> *New Direction Weight Control System*
> Wabash County Hospital, Wabash, IN

※ ※ ※ ※ ※

"My psychiatrist says I have a persecution complex, but she's just saying that because she hates me."

※ ※ ※ ※ ※

A visitor to New York City was taking a stroll in Central Park when a well-dressed man came up to him and asked for $4.00 for a cup of coffee.

The visitor looked at him and said, "Nobody's gonna give you that much for a cup of coffee. You'd be a lot better off asking for 50 cents."

"Look," said the well-dressed bum, "either give me the $4.00 or go away, but don't tell me how to run my business."

❋ ❋ ❋ ❋ ❋

A vacation is that brief period of time between trying to get ahead so you can leave and trying to catch up when you get back.

❋ ❋ ❋ ❋ ❋

Offices are great places for graffiti. Just consider this one where the manager had placed this sign on the bulletin board: TODAY IS THE TOMORROW YOU WORRIED ABOUT YESTERDAY.
Beneath it was a bit of graffiti: AND NOW YOU KNOW WHY.

❋ ❋ ❋ ❋ ❋

A lot of maturing takes place between "It fell" and "I dropped it."

❋ ❋ ❋ ❋ ❋

"Doctor, do you recall telling me to ease up, to take it slower, to get me some women and to do some carousing? To generally ease up?"
"Yes, I do. And did you take my advice?"
"I did. In spades! But tell me now. . .how do I get my business back?"

❋ ❋ ❋ ❋ ❋

That guy conceited? Well, he's my boss. Every time he looks in the mirror, he bows!

❋ ❋ ❋ ❋ ❋

My boss is really a hard SOB. The other day an employee came in late and the boss said: "Where the hell have you been! You're an hour late!"
"I fell down the stairs at home," the fellow replied.
"What! And that took an entire hour?"

"I've been so damned tired lately," the boss said, "that I can't burn the candle at either end."

✳ ✳ ✳ ✳ ✳

Our boss has a strange sense of humor. He gets on the elevator that's packed and says loudly, "Gotta go! Gotta go!'" Then he sighs and says, "Oops!" And sometimes he'll just burp loudly, look up inquiringly, then says, "tasty" or "um-m-m, good!"

✳ ✳ ✳ ✳ ✳

The customer is the goose that lays the golden egg. Management's job is to get him to lay it in our direction!

Don't worry about complaints because as long as you have customers, you'll have them. . .unless you're an undertaker. But, come to think of it, they have them, too. Consider Lazarus.

✳ ✳ ✳ ✳ ✳

Many large corporations simply cannot stand prosperity. Fortunately, most don't have to.

✳ ✳ ✳ ✳ ✳

The secretary went to her boss in tears. He seated her and asked what was wrong. "No money," she sobbed. "We're broke. I've been looking for a new job and three companies want me."

"What! Three companies want you!" the boss exploded in alarm. "But I need you here. What three companies want you?"

"Light, telephone and water!"

✳ ✳ ✳ ✳ ✳

Failure is the path of least persistence.

The boss's secretary criticizes everybody in the place. Nobody is exempt from her caustic tongue. When Santa Claus appeared at last year's office party, she told him to shave, to wear more conservative clothes and to lose weight.

* * * * *

Samson truly hit the nail on the head when he took two columns and brought down the house. Now *that's* advertising!

* * * * *

The boss's assistant is an arrogant stuffed shirt, the very living proof that stuffed shirts come in all sizes.

* * * * *

You know you've got employee relations problems when:
. . .The employees refer to the parking lot as "the demilitarized zone."
. . .You find out your employees have developed first-strike nuclear capabilities.

* * * * *

Pete Frazier was the worst businessman in town. Why, he took bankruptcy twice and didn't make a cent either time.

* * * * *

Paying off your creditors after you've gone out of business is old-fashioned. Why, it's like making your regular house payments after it has burned down.

* * * * *

The president of the company addressed the Board of Directors at the annual meeting. "Gentlemen," he began, "I wish to report that this year's annual report is now being brought to you in color. . .RED!"

One of the nicest, sweetest, most endearing forms of flattery in the business world is. . .a raise!

✻ ✻ ✻ ✻ ✻

George Smith seems very young to be one of our company's vice-presidents. And when he writes his memos, he *really* seems young. They're in crayon!

✻ ✻ ✻ ✻ ✻

I worked like a dog to make my company solvent. Then just as I managed to put two ends together and had them meet, somebody moved the ends.

✻ ✻ ✻ ✻ ✻

The officers of the company were having a discussion on how to get employees to work on time. The first vice-president had this suggestion: "Why don't we reduce the number of employee parking spaces from 200 to 185?"
All nodded in agreement. "That'll do it," said the president.

✻ ✻ ✻ ✻ ✻

My boss came in from lunch, took off his tie and handed it to me. It had an enormous spot on it. He said, "I've just learned that a new tie always attracts the soup of the day!"

✻ ✻ ✻ ✻ ✻

The chemical manufacturing company was having an executive meeting to discuss how to meet government standards on waste disposal. And they weren't getting anywhere at all. Finally, one man said: "Our situation reminds me of the Bible story about Moses running from the Egyptians. Moses prayed to God for help and was told there was good news and bad news. "The good news," intoned the voice from on high, "is that I will part the sea for you so that you and all your people can cross the Red Sea safely."
"Tell me the bad news," said Moses.
"The bad news," said God, "is that you'll have to file an environmental impact statement!"

A reporter had arranged an interview with one of the richest men in the world. . .Mr. J. Paul Getty. He walked into Getty's office and asked, "If you were out of the business now, would you consider that you'd be worth as much as a billion dollars?"

"You could say that," Getty replied, "but you've got to remember that a billion dollars doesn't go nearly as far as it used to."

* * * * *

My boss returned from his thirtieth class reunion and said, "If you think things improve with age, don't attend a class reunion because it'll sure change your mind."

* * * * *

The guy was known as the hardest-working executive in the business. . .he just never quit work. But now he was in the waiting room of the maternity ward expecting his wife to give birth. While he waited, he furiously worked on a sheaf of papers that he'd taken from his briefcase.

After a couple of hours, a nurse entered the room and announced to him: "Sir, it's a girl."

"Well," snapped the guy, "ask her what she wants."

* * * * *

Most successful businessmen have learned that executives, like automobiles, don't run by themselves, except downhill.

* * * * *

After operating for some months on an unofficial overdraft, our company got this letter from the bank. "Gentlemen: We would feel most accommodated if we could return to the old system when YOU banked with US."

* * * * *

Reports to higher executives are like bikinis. What they reveal is interesting but what they conceal is vital.

A wise old man, the founder of a very successful enterprise, remarked to his assistant: "I tell you, George, today you've got stocks going sky-high! And you've got to be selling either a copier or a contraceptive. It's reproduction or no reproduction and not a dadblamed thing in between!"

❋ ❋ ❋ ❋ ❋

In diplomacy, they call it a communiqué, the military call it a dispatch, while in business it's a memo. But everywhere else they are more direct and honest. . .they call it bull––!

❋ ❋ ❋ ❋ ❋

"I had one heckuva hard time when I first started my business," the merchant said to a friend.
"Why was that?" asked the friend.
"Well, I guess the reason was that I started on a shoestring when everyone started wearing loafers."

❋ ❋ ❋ ❋ ❋

Eddie Fletcher had just been made a vice-president of his company and was he tickled! He was telling–bragging a bit–of his promotion, only to hear his friend say: "A vice-presidency doesn't mean a danged thing! They're a dime a dozen today. Heck, my supermarket has a vice-president in charge of beans."
This seemed a lie to the new vice-president, so he called that same supermarket and asked for the vice-president in charge of beans. The voice on the phone asked: "Canned, frozen or fresh?"

❋ ❋ ❋ ❋ ❋

The only man who ever got all his work done by Friday, was Robinson Crusoe.

❋ ❋ ❋ ❋ ❋

Peter Alkent was president of a small manufacturing company. He was also an avid amateur painter, always studying art and taking lessons. But he was growing old, so he decided to give all his own paintings to a charity. But which one? He went to the company lawyer to seek advice and posed the question to him:

"Which charity to give your paintings to, eh? Hm-m," the lawyer paused, thinking hard. "Why don't you try the Altgeld Association for the Blind?"

* * * * *

Executive to traveling salesman for the company: "Emil, I can't approve this expense account. But I tell you what. . .I'd like to buy the fiction rights to it!"

* * * * *

The two secretaries were having an argument over capital punishment, whether it was necessary or not. A friend from a nearby office came by their table and they asked: "Ellen, we can't decide whether capital punishment is a good thing or not. What do you think?"

"I favor it. . .but only if it isn't too severe."

* * * * *

A large defense plant needed an assistant to the chief accountant. The advertisement read: "This is not an executive position, therefore, necessitates considerable work."

* * * * *

For years, our office wondered why before he signed a paper, our personnel manager would open his desk drawer, glance inside it, close it and then sign. One time when he was sick at home, we decided to see what was in that drawer. So we opened it and there was a slip of paper on which was written, "2 Ns. . .1L."

* * * * *

They tell the story about Thomas Edison and his factory, in which he had just one large clock. Mr. Edison noticed that employees spent too much time watching the clock, so his solution to their wasting all this time was to install several more clocks, all with different times. Of course, soon the workers tired of trying to figure out what time it really was and the trouble for Mr. Edison was ended. . .by his ingenuity.

✳ ✳ ✳ ✳ ✳

He's my boss and he's typical of most of them. When he talks to you, he often says, "I know that I have my faults but. . .being wrong is not one of them!"

✳ ✳ ✳ ✳ ✳

Here's a little poem that typifies the usual egotist:
Hurrah for the guy who is wisest and best,
Cheers to the man whose judgment is blest.
Hurrah to the man who's shrewd as can be,
I cheer the man who agrees with me.

✳ ✳ ✳ ✳ ✳

If you want a good formula for success, try aspiration, inspiration and perspiration.

✳ ✳ ✳ ✳ ✳

Three executives were arguing over the luncheon check. "I'll take it," one said, "I can write it off my income tax."
The second one said, "No! No! Let me have it. I can charge it to my company."
"No! No! No!" said the third executive. "I'll take it. I'm filing for bankruptcy tomorrow."

✳ ✳ ✳ ✳ ✳

Our company has come on hard times. We are cutting back on all expenses. Even our president, at lunch, orders a domestic Zinfandel.

✳ ✳ ✳ ✳ ✳

My boss is terribly overweight but he's too lazy to exercise. The doctor told him he wouldn't live many years if he didn't exercise and lose weight. So, he decided to do both. He dieted quite well but in terms of exercise, he hired–would you believe it, a valet-jogger!

27

Mark Twain hit the nail on the head when he said: "It usually takes more than three weeks to prepare a good impromptu speech."

✳ ✳ ✳ ✳ ✳

Second Executive Vice-President: "I just finished my art class at the local Art Institute, George. Here's my best painting. Everybody I showed it to said they thought it was a wow!"

First Vice-President: "I agree. . .almost. I'd call it the wowsiest painting I every saw!"

✳ ✳ ✳ ✳ ✳

This conceited cuss has carried on a love affair for years ...with himself.

✳ ✳ ✳ ✳ ✳

There is a bank officer on whose desk is a sign reading: "In this office, the single word 'NO' is a complete sentence."

✳ ✳ ✳ ✳ ✳

Our boss has an enormous office–real fancy, full of great furniture. It's so big he can play racket ball in it without moving a single piece of furniture. And that's not all. It has space for sleeping ten people and that makes it perfect for staff meetings.

The boss's desk is really huge. . .has its own zip code! It's so big that, one time, a confused pilot mistook it for a Kennedy Airport runway. And the carpeting? Well, suffice it to say that anyone under 5'1" would disappear walking across it!

✳ ✳ ✳ ✳ ✳

Just outside the office of the chief controller for a major automobile company, there is a sign that reads: "There is no such thing as petty cash!"

Pray that mini skirts don't return. If they do, some women executives will have to ask for early retirement.

* * * * *

Some male executives are male chauvinist pigs, or, as John Wayne used to put it: "The woman's place is in the home and she ought to go there just as soon as she's off work!"

* * * * *

"George, we've got the best firm of lawyers in Chicago. Why, they are unbeatable. The other night, a burglar broke into their office and lost five hundred bucks of his own money!"

"Jackson had to skip the meeting, he's being sentenced today."

Did you hear about the president of a cereal company who combined love of art with extreme show-offism? He bought a truly fine painting for $500,000 and hung both the painting and the beautifully *framed canceled check* in his office!

✳ ✳ ✳ ✳ ✳

The foreman is the man in charge. He tells shipping where the product should go. He tells manufacturing where spare parts should go and, every now and then, he tells management where it can go.

✳ ✳ ✳ ✳ ✳

Our sales manager is seventy-five years old. And he's really a whiz. The other day, while in Detroit, he was getting ready for bed in his hotel room when there was a knock on his door. He opened it and there stood a lovely, beautifully-dressed young woman. "Oh, I'm sorry," she said, "I must have the wrong room."

"No, young lady," he said, "you've got the right room but you're thirty years too late."

✳ ✳ ✳ ✳ ✳

My boss died last month. A good man with only one fault. He was cheap! Cheap! Cheap! They tell me he died of onebarculosis.

✳ ✳ ✳ ✳ ✳

To paraphrase Winston Churchill's description of an able politician: "Executive ability is the ability to foretell what is going to happen tomorrow, next week, next month and next year. . .and the ability to explain why it didn't happen."

✳ ✳ ✳ ✳ ✳

Old Jake Orens was so superstitious that he wouldn't read a book through if it contained a Chapter 11.

The company was losing money and needed help. So they called in a consultant who began to question all the employees. He asked one junior executive: "What do you do?"

The executive replied: "Practically nothing."

He asked another ranked employee the same question and got a similar reply. "Nothing much."

The consultant made his report. "Too much duplication of work."

※ ※ ※ ※ ※

My job is almost impossible. It's my boss! He docks me if I'm a minute late. And if I'm ten minutes early, he charges me rent!

※ ※ ※ ※ ※

The aggressive vice-president was surveying the company's entire operation. He started with the shipping department, walking toward the door of the warehouse. There he saw a young man leaning against a post, reading a newspaper. "How much do you make a week?" he asked the lad.

"Two hundred dollars, Sir" was the reply.

"Here's a week's pay," the executive said. "Now get out!" The executive walked on until he met the foreman. "How long has that kid worked here?" he asked the foreman.

"He doesn't work here. . .he was waiting for a receipt for the merchandise he delivered!"

※ ※ ※ ※ ※

Our boss is so uppity and haughty he doesn't have a secretary. No, Sir! Not him. He's too conceited. He's got a handmaiden.

※ ※ ※ ※ ※

The first vice-president of our company is a woman. And she is the perennial bitch. . .impossible to get along with. Why, she was returning from a business trip when the airport was overcrowded with incoming planes. They put her broomstick in a holding pattern!

"When two men in business always agree. . .one of them is unnecessary."
William Wrigley, Jr.

* * * * *

We all know the type of executive who is always trying to look better, if not different, than God intended him to look. Sam Jones, for example, got a toupee to cover his baldness, had a face-lift, got his teeth capped, and got his ears pinned back. Well, he just looked swell! And was he pleased with himself. Then one morning, driving to work, he had a terrible collision and went flying out of the car and rolling down the street, losing his teeth, his toupee, his face-lift. . .every change he'd made. In desperation, he turned to look upward. "Dear God," he moaned, "how could you do this terrible thing to me, faithful me?"

There was a pause, then a voice came from on high. "To tell you the honest truth, Sam, I didn't recognize you!"

* * * * *

He was probably the cheapest son of an unwed mother in all Chicago. You want proof? Note this: He took a cab to his bankruptcy court proceedings and then invited the cab driver in as a creditor.

* * * * *

One of the best examples of an explanation of the difference between faith and belief is the tale of the boss who was explaining just that. . .the difference between faith and belief to his employees. "If I go to the circus and see a tightrope walker with a wheelbarrow start across it, that's belief. If I sit in the wheelbarrow while he pushes it across the tightrope. . .that's faith."

* * * * *

Tommy Brown is a business consultant. He describes his job as "the sort of work where they call you in at the last minute to share the blame."

Finally, the boss asked his secretary to tone down her clothing, to wear less provocative things.

"But I dress conservatively," she exclaimed. "What makes you say I don't."

"Because," he explained, "in the course of the past year, I've seen every ass-pect of your anatomy except your ears!"

✳ ✳ ✳ ✳ ✳

My company watches every penny! Here's an example. They did put a shower in the executive washroom, but then they put in pay toilets to cover the cost of the showers!

✳ ✳ ✳ ✳ ✳

Some say that President Coolidge was a good but humorless president. But he had the wit to say, when asked why he did not want to run for a second term: "Why, because in this job, there's no chance for advancement."

✳ ✳ ✳ ✳ ✳

Tax loopholes are like parking spaces: They all disappear before you get there.

✳ ✳ ✳ ✳ ✳

"My boss inherited over two million dollars. . .then he lost it all."

"How sad. How did he lose it?"

"He invested every last penny of it in. . .U.S. Blondes!"

✳ ✳ ✳ ✳ ✳

He's the most unreasonable boss I ever had. Why, he's the kinda jerk who'd ask the Venus de Milo for elbow room!

✳ ✳ ✳ ✳ ✳

"You'll have to talk to the department head."

"I refuse. I don't want to talk to the disembodied."

(May the saints preserve us from the literal-minded!)

Of course, my boss knows money can't buy happiness, doesn't everybody?   His problem is that he loves money more than happiness.

* * * * *

After church, the pastor greeted Eddie Jones, saying, "Ah, Mr. Jones, I'm really glad to see you here."
"I'm glad to be here. After all, money isn't everything."
"Well, well, and who told you that?"
"My boss."

* * * * *

Alone, wealth can't bring you happiness,
Wealth alone can't make us glad,
So might's well take a chance, why not,
At being rich and sad.

* * * * *

The biblical Noah was, among other things, a very successful businessman.   When the entire world was in liquidation, that feller Noah floated his own company.

* * * * *

There is a certain magic that accompanies some words. Consider the term: CONSULTANT.   There must be a mystique about that word because the president of one company paid a consultant $300 an hour for the same advice given him time after time by his assistant.

* * * * *

Our best secretary just had a baby and named him Boss... because that's where she got him.

* * * * *

The guy was in a hurry, jumped into a cab that proceeded at a snail's pace, stopping time after time for red lights, packed traffic, and so on.   Desperately impatient, the passenger shouted: "Cabbie, can't you go any faster?"

"Sure I can," the cabbie said, "but I'm not allowed to leave the cab."

* * * * *

The problem or trouble with wishful thinking in business is that it is usually 90 percent wishful and 10 percent thinking.

* * * * *

The founder of the company was 90 years old and the entire staff thought it would be a great idea to give a party for him. And they did. The old man had come up from Florida for the party and the staff had arranged a room for him in the city's finest hotel, to which the old man retired after the party. When he unlocked the door to his room, he was greeted by a lovely blonde in a negligee, who smiled at him, saying, "Come on in, you handsome man, you. We'll have a grand night. How about some super sex."

The old man thought a minute, then replied: "Soup!"

* * * * *

My boss was at a business meeting when he passed out. The others brought him to. Then they brought him two more and he was fine.

* * * * *

One must be very careful about signs in an office. I recall the one place where the boss put up a sign that said: DO IT NOW! The sign company stopped by and asked him if the sign had been effective.

"You bet!" said the boss. "Too effective. My accountant skedaddled with $50,000. My assistant ran off with my private secretary, our two key clerks quit, and every night when I went to get my car in the company parking lot, I found all four tires flat!"

My boss went on a diet at last! Well, he lost ten pounds because he could only eat vegetables and drink wine. Oh yes. . .he also lost his driver's license.

✳ ✳ ✳ ✳ ✳

The boss's secretary complained to him that he never told her where he was going or when he'd be back. She asked him to let her know these things before he left. He said, "You don't need to know all that stuff." But she wouldn't give up. So he gave her the following instructions:

"If they call early in the morning, say: 'He hasn't come in yet.'"

Later, say: "He hasn't come in yet."

A bit later: "I expect him any minute."

A lot later: "He just called and said he'd be late."

Then: "He was in but now he's away from his desk. I don't know where."

After that: "He's gone to lunch."

Later: "He's due back any minute."

Once more: "He's not back yet. Can I take a message?"

Then: "He's someplace in our offices. I know 'cause his coat is here."

Later: "He's gone again. And I can't tell you when he'll be back."

Finally: "Sure sorry, but he's gone for the day."

✳ ✳ ✳ ✳ ✳

This gal was a vice-president of her company and was she snooty. Why, her nose was turned up so high she blew her hat off when she sneezed.

✳ ✳ ✳ ✳ ✳

An optimistic executive is one who figures that what's for sure going to be, will be. . .postponed.

✳ ✳ ✳ ✳ ✳

The manager of a department store men's furnishings department and his assistant caught a salesman stealing from the cash register. The manager was going to fire the clerk at once but his assistant stopped him, saying: "Let's face it, Sir. We all started out on a small scale ourselves."

* * * * *

A pessimist is just an optimist who's got more information.

* * * * *

A huge new computer was doing most of the work in the office of a prominent insurance company. Nobody could find what went wrong so they called in a consultant from the manufacturer. He took only a moment to open his bag, take out a hammer and tap the side of the computer. Miraculously, it started working!

After that the consultant made out his bill for $750! The office manager was really upset, saying: "What a gyp. Why, you didn't do a damned thing except tap on that bastard machine with your hammer!"

"You didn't read the bill carefully," the consultant said. "Here!"

He took the bill and read. . ."Gently tapping the computer with the hammer - $50.00. Knowing where to tap - $700.00!"

* * * * *

If at first you don't succeed. . .you're sure average.

* * * * *

Johnny Fortunato was the protege of the owner of a large electronics company. The man had put Johnny through five years of college, saw him get his MBA, and now Johnny was ready to join the business. His benefactor sat him down in the office and said: "Johnny, it's imperative that you remember that honesty is the best policy here. And I want you to continue working on your degree in corporate law. Why? Because you will be simply astonished at what you can do and still be honest!"

A wit once put this business statement together: "The gods gave us fire to invent the fire engine. And they gave us ambition so we could invent bankruptcy court."

* * * * *

Jealousy among a company's officers is not at all uncommon. Consider this exchange between two vice-presidents of the same company who were constantly trying to top one another. The one guy bought a car phone and, naturally, the other guy had to do the same thing. As soon as he had one, he called his rival and said: "Howdy, Joe, I'm calling from my car."

The other said: "Hold on a moment, will you? I've got a call on the other line."

* * * * *

What constitutes a capable executive for a business today? Perhaps this: He or she is the sort of person who can take a two-hour lunch and not diminish his firm's production.

* * * * *

Isn't it a truism that American idealism all too often means being willing to make any sacrifice so long as it doesn't hurt business!

* * * * *

It was an extremely stressful job and Mary Eldridge was having a hard time going to sleep nights. She asked her doctor what to do and he prescribed sleeping pills.

"But, Doctor, they don't work for me. I've tried them time after time. Maybe you could allow me some of those pills they give pregnant women. I hear they work very well."

"You don't want those, Miss Eldridge. They are just for labor."

"But, Doctor, don't you have anything for management?"

There are more than a few executives who could make the statement George Burns made about retirement: "I'll never retire because there isn't a thing I can't do now that I didn't do at 18."

* * * * *

The company's chief executive was having a meeting with all the junior executives and was telling them about the new man about to join the company. "As you know," he began, "Mr. Sloane, who owns our company, has his son coming to work here tomorrow. But we are all directed to offer the lad no special privileges or considerations. So I enjoin you to treat him just as you would any other newcomer to the business. . .who was due to take it over in a year or two!"

* * * * *

"Y'know," one guy said to another, "I always figured on my son sharing my business. But, y'know what. . .the government beat him to it!"

* * * * *

Three guys from the office were having a drink together and discussing the boss. "He's OK," said one fellow. "But I can't stand his breath when he talks to me. It's terrible. Stinks! I understand they pushed him over three times last Halloween!"

* * * * *

The ultimate, indispensable six inches to success lies between your ears.

* * * * *

A tough-looking old guy walked into the office of a charitable organization and told the receptionist: "I'd like to see the dumb bastard who runs this outfit."

The receptionist gasped. "Sir, if you wish to speak to someone in this organization, you must ask with respect and courtesy. Now. . .who was it you wished to see?"

"I already told you. I want to see the dumb bastard who runs the show here."

"Sir! I told you that you must speak with respect. Don't use that kind of language. I won't tell them you are here unless you do. Now, Sir, whom did you wish to see?"

"The dumb schlemiel who runs the show here, that's who!"

"For. . .the. . .last. . .time. The name, please!"

"Look, Sis. I'm a rich guy and I want to give a million bucks to your organization to help in the good work they do. But I'll not do it unless I can talk with the dumb bastard who runs the show. Got that?"

The receptionist turns her head to see the chief executive come toward her desk. She turns to the old coot and says: "Here comes the dumb bastard who runs this show. I'll introduce you, Sir!"

✳ ✳ ✳ ✳ ✳

Still another type of executive can always see the bright side of trouble. . .somebody else's trouble!

✳ ✳ ✳ ✳ ✳

Joe Spitale migrated to this country while in his teens. After a lifetime of hard work, he was made president of his company and they honored him with a presentation dinner. After dinner, Joe was asked to speak. "Friends," he began, "when I came here I didn't have a nickel in my pocket. Yet I now owe the banks $1,500,000!"

✳ ✳ ✳ ✳ ✳

Two executives were discussing the high price of hotels in New York City. "I suppose $75 for a meal isn't all that bad," one of them said, "but for a continental breakfast?"

✳ ✳ ✳ ✳ ✳

There was a most unusual event at our convention. The speaker rode into the convention, down the aisle and up to the podium on a white horse. It was the first time a *complete* horse had appeared at the podium!

I had one heluva time at our last convention. It was held at a nudist colony and was just great. . .all except pulling off the name tag.

"ACTUALLY, I WAS HOPING YOU'D PUT IT ALL ON THE DOOR."

This executive always went to the annual convention of his business associates. He was especially fond of the costume ball that followed. One year his wife got him a dog costume for the event, which he happily packed when he left for the convention. Of course, he said, spouses were not invited.

Well, this year the wife decided to go anyway. She bought a bunny costume for herself, got on the train and headed for Chicago, the convention site.

At the ball, she spotted her masked husband in his costume and went to him, began a conversation and they hit it off from the start. He asked her to spend the night with him and she agreed, providing they'd not remove their masks.

When both got home, she asked if had a good time. He said he had but that he didn't have time to go to the ball and had lent his doggy costume to his friend, Paul, who claimed he'd had the best time of his life.

* * * * *

The teacher asked the class if anyone could name the seasons. The son of a prominent dress manufacturer held up his hand. "Yes, Aaron," the teacher said.

"Busy and Slack!" Aaron responded.

* * * * *

The boss asked his secretary to wear clothing a bit less sexy.

"But my dress is NOT sexy," the girl exploded. "I dress for comfort only!"

"Maybe so," the boss said. "But can you explain why every time you bend over to put something in the lowest file case drawer, the fire alarm goes off?"

* * * * *

My boss is the company's official cheapskate. He guards his money like an FBI agent. You can always pick him out in a restaurant. He's the one sitting with his back to the check!

* * * * *

Our president once stopped at a bar while on his way home from work. He ordered a shot of scotch.

After drinking it, he ordered another. When served, he asked the server: "Are you the owner?"

"Sure am."

"I'm a businessman and I've got an idea that could double the drinks you serve in here. Want to hear it?"

"Sure do," replied the bartender. "I'd really appreciate that."

"Good. Now will you let me off my bill if I tell you?"

"Yep!" replied the barkeep. And he tore up the bill. "So tell me now. . .how can I double the amount of liquor I sell?"

Our president stood up. "Just fill up the glasses," he said and then walked out.

※ ※ ※ ※ ※

A positive attitude is absolutely essential and the best, fastest way to move up the corporate ladder. . .unless the boss has a single daughter.

※ ※ ※ ※ ※

"How do you explain your extraordinary success as a door-to-door salesman?" a newcomer asked the experienced oldster.

"Oh, that's easy to tell you. When I ring the bell and a woman comes to the door, I ask: 'Hi, Sis, is your mother home?'"

※ ※ ※ ※ ※

If someone falls off the corporate ladder, it's not thought of as a tragedy so much as a job opening.

※ ※ ※ ※ ※

My boss was a really mean guy. Everybody hated him for the tyrant he was. Then all of a sudden, he died. At the funeral, as the casket was being lowered, a huge clap of thunder with lightning sounded. "Well, I guess he got there," his secretary sighed.

※ ※ ※ ※ ※

It's a paramount rule that executives should not cheat at their jobs. The way to avoid that sin is to get it all out of your system at your weekly golf game.

※ ※ ※ ※ ※

A New York executive loved to play the stock market. But he lost all his savings and now stood at a hotel window ready to jump.

"Don't!" a voice told him.

"But I've lost everything," the startled executive replied. "Why shouldn't I?"

Again the voice spoke: "Borrow $500. Call your broker and buy wheat."

He did and the price of wheat tripled in five days. That night the same voice told him to buy soybeans. He did and within a week the price of wheat quadrupled. So the man did the same thing for several weeks. Boy, was he riding high. He had close to $500,000.

Next he heard the same voice tell him, "Quit! Don't invest another cent. . .in anything!" But he couldn't resist. He plowed it all back in the grain market and lost it all. Every. . .last. . .penny!"

He stood, once again, in front of the window on the fifteenth floor. "What'll I do now, oh Know-it-all?" he moaned.

"JUMP!" the voice said.

❋ ❋ ❋ ❋ ❋

Experience is the comb that life gives you after you lose your hair.

❋ ❋ ❋ ❋ ❋

As John Feldhauser walked out of the station headed for a cab to take him to his appointment, he met another guy waiting for a cab. John asked him: "Why don't we share a cab, Mister? Cheaper that way."

"OK by me," the man said. "When he gets here, you take the tires and I'll take the transmission."

❋ ❋ ❋ ❋ ❋

Bankruptcy is only a legal proceeding where you place your money in your pants and give your coat to your creditors (on a hot summer day).

❋ ❋ ❋ ❋ ❋

A group of executives were sitting around the conference table and they were furious at the boss. After most had complained to him, he responded: "I need more time to do what we agreed to do. After all, if you put a bull out with a bunch of cows, you wouldn't expect to see a barnlot full of calves the very next morning, would you?"

One executive responded: "No, but we would expect to see a barnlot full of contented cows."

* * * * *

Isn't it strange that they never ask a man how he combines HIS business with HIS marriage?

* * * * *

The sales manager was holding a meeting of his salesmen. "After the way you guys performed last year, such a lousy total sales, I now understand just why our new high-rise office buildings can't have open windows."

* * * * *

As the song has it, "Diamonds are a Girl's Best Friend." And for a man. . .a dog is best. Now you know which sex has the most sense.

* * * * *

About the ever-popular business conference, Fred Allen had a neat description: "A conference is a gathering of important people who singly can do nothing, but together decide that nothing can be done."

* * * * *

Jerry Portnoy had a bit too much to drink while attending his convention. Suddenly, he disappeared and when the boss asked where he was, a fellow worker said, "He's outside in the parking lot posing as a speed bump."

* * * * *

It is axiomatic that today a woman in business must be twice as capable as a man. Luckily, that's not difficult.

A bunch of junior executives were sitting around a table in a bar, having a pre-home cocktail and discussing their bosses.

"My boss has an ego so big," one of them said, "that last week, coming out of a McDonald's, he got his head stuck in the golden arch!"

* * * * *

The one important thing I have learned over the years is the difference between taking one's work seriously and taking one's self seriously. The first is imperative and the second is disastrous.

Margot Fonteyn
The Laughter Prescription Newletter
Carlsbad, CA 92009

* * * * *

Ask anybody saddled with the responsibility of paying off creditors after their firm has gone out of business. The general opinion is that it is something like leaving the TV set on after you've fallen asleep.

* * * * *

David Sarnoff once said: "Competition brings out the best in products but the worst in people."

* * * * *

A board of directors member once asked just why the company needed to hire a consultant and just what it was that a consultant did. A staff member answered his question. "He's the kind of guy who takes the wristwatch off you and then tells you what time it is."

* * * * *

This guy was promoted over twenty-five of his fellow workers. He called a meeting of them to announce his policies. "I am not going to change," he told them, "but all of you had better do so."

The retired past president of our company was invited to address the board of directors and to give his ideas about the future of American business. He opened his talk by saying: "Be careful. Most Americans today drive last year's car, wear this year's clothes, and live on next year's income."

* * * * *

Someone put it most aptly: "Worry is the interest you pay on trouble before it's due."

* * * * *

Jamie Thomas came shivering into the office on a bitter-cold January morning. His secretary remarked: "It sure is cold, isn't it!"
He replied: "You don't know the half of it. Why there was a flasher just outside our building and he walked up to a woman and merely described himself!"

* * * * *

Economics is the study of how limited resources can best be made to serve absolutely unlimited American wants.

* * * * *

If she wants to get ahead in today's business world, a woman must look like a girl, act like a lady, think like a man, fight like a cat, and work like a dog.

* * * * *

Johnny Edwards moved up in his company fast. Soon he became a vice-president and he planned to retire within two years, but the bankruptcy court beat him to it.

* * * * *

The new secretary stood in front of the paper shredder looking upset and confused. An experienced woman happened by, saw the girl's confusion, and asked if she could help.
"I guess I don't know how to work this machine," said the

new girl. "Could you show me how?"

The older woman took the papers from the new employee and put them through the shredder. "See? That's how it works," she said.

"Oh, thanks a million," the new girl said. "Now show me where the copies come out, will you?"

* * * * *

Our lady vice-president is known as "marryin'" Jill. Why, she's been married so many times, her face is pocked with rice marks.

* * * * *

Delegating responsibility is a tricky way to turn something over to someone else because you don't know how to do it without letting any other person know you don't know!

* * * * *

THE BUSINESS MAN

This personage (who's mostly tired),
The business man, is much admired;
Yet not for worlds would I be he
Who may not loaf and brood like me,
Upon the whyness of the isness,
But has to buckle down to business,
The crux of which, from all I hear,
Is buying cheap and selling dear–
And that's hard work; and so, my client
(In England called "The Weary Giant")
To get some rest must often go
And see a whirly-girly Show.

The Mirthful Lyre by Arthur Guiterman
Harper & Brothers Publishers
New York & London: 1918.

* * * * *

The art of being a boss is the art of knowing what to overlook.

MEGA
INDUSTRIES

*"IF ANYONE WANTS ME, I'LL BE OUT PRICING
POLITICANS."*

If our executive vice-president were asked to name the three most brilliant, effective, and capable vice-presidents in the nation, he'd have a hard time naming the other two.

✳ ✳ ✳ ✳ ✳

My company isn't known for its ability to plan ahead. By the time it had put up its new office building in the suburbs, the suburbs had moved twenty-five miles further out.

✳ ✳ ✳ ✳ ✳

No man is a true, hundred-percent success until his mother-in-law admits it.

Two friends, both quite beautiful, were having lunch together. One of them had recently married a stockbroker and her friend asked just how she had met him. "Oh," replied the recent bride, "we were introduced by a mutual fund."

✳ ✳ ✳ ✳ ✳

EARLY TO BED AND LATE TO RISE
Don Herold

I've decided that getting up and going to work is just a form of nervousness, so I keep calm and stay in bed. It takes arrogance and courage, but I stay right there until I get some work done. Then I may go down to my office and play.

When I say play, I mean dictating letters, answering the telephone, holding "conferences" and doing those other office chores that most people call work.

One of the reasons I stay adamantly in bed in the a.m. is that I am an unusually energetic person, without a lazy bone in my body, and my natural impulses are to leap up, shave and dress in a jiffy, rush to the office, and start the day busily, achieving practically nothing. Instead, I force myself to start what I consider real work at seven o'clock or eight, or whenever I wake up, and to stay at it and finish it before I waste any pep on the useless, unimportant, conventional movements of rising and getting to an office, or distracting myself with the morning paper and the morning mail.

I never look at my mail until afternoon. Looking at the mail first thing in the morning is nothing but sheer boyish curiosity, mixed with a certain amount of laziness. A man who attends to his morning mail in the morning is letting other people decide how he is to spend his day. (I've observed over the years that most people accomplish little more every day than getting up and going to work.)

I tell myself that my work is somewhat mental, and that a person can come nearer to being 100 percent mental in bed than anywhere else. His calluses don't chafe, his shoes don't hurt, the angle of the chair does not annoy him, he does not have to figure what to do with his arms or legs. If he has a brain, he's practically nothing but brain. . .in bed.

Another advantage is that bed is the one place in the world where other people leave a man alone. People somehow regard bedrooms as sacred territory and do not, as a rule, crash in uninvited. Furthermore, people feel that a normal man in bed fairly late in the morning must be sick, perhaps with something infectious. Let 'em think so!

Ruskin was grasping for a seclusion similar to that which bed gives when, upon entering on a serious spell of work, he sent out cards reading: "Mr J. Ruskin is about to begin a work of great importance and therefore begs that in reference to calls and correspondence, you will consider him dead for the next two months."

Mark Twain was, of course, the patron saint of all bed workers. He was a sensationally sensible man, and he saw no point in getting up to write.

A more recent advocate of bed work was Winston Churchill, who remained in bed until late in the a.m., and went to bed again after lunch and, I believe, again later in the day. Thanks to this conservation of energy, he lived into his hearty nineties.

Another famous bed worker was Rossini, the composer. There is a story that once, while composing an opera in bed, he dropped one of the arias on the floor and it slid some distance away. Instead of getting up to retrieve it, he merely wrote a new aria.

It is said Voltaire did most of his scribbling in bed, and that Disraeli wrote some of his greatest speeches while stretched out on the floor. And lawyer Louis Nizer says, "I prefer to work from a reclining position. Even my office chair tilts, and a hidden footrest permits me to recline sufficiently, without offending my client's notion of dignity. I have found justification for my lazy posture in medical journals which suggest that it takes strain off the heart and increases stamina as well as thinking powers."

My own theory is that an office is one of the least efficient inventions of modern man, and that it should be stayed out of as much as possible. If housewives only knew how most executive husbands fritter away their days, their awe of "Father at the office" would become one more shattered schoolgirl illusion. Most men get more real work done on their trips and vacations than they do all the rest of the year.

My regimen of relaxation brings all sorts of shame on my head. I am called a laggard, a bum, an escapist; I've also been accused of suffering from habitual hangovers. Perhaps I may even be accused of working for the Associated Mattress Manufacturers of America: if they can get everybody to spend 25 percent more time in bed, it will eventually boost mattress sales 25 percent. That's all right with me. What's good for the Associated Mattress Manufacturers is good for the country.

✳ ✳ ✳ ✳ ✳

Executive secretary to boss: "A voice crying in the wilderness would like to speak to you. I believe it's your son."

✳ ✳ ✳ ✳ ✳

A couple Iowa City stockbrokers were having lunch. One said, "Let's not talk business today."
The other said, "OK by me. Let's talk about women."
"Good! Common or preferred?"

✳ ✳ ✳ ✳ ✳

Business executive to salesman: "You've got a good approach. Now let's see how you depart!"

✳ ✳ ✳ ✳ ✳

Two junior executives were having a discussion over coffee: "I asked my shrink to show me one positive result from all my visits to his office."
"Interesting," said the other executive. "What did he say?"
"He didn't say anything. He showed me his new Porsche!"

✳ ✳ ✳ ✳ ✳

Homecoming husband to wife: "Whew! I took an aptitude test this afternoon. Thank goodness I own the company!"

✳ ✳ ✳ ✳ ✳

"But I just gave you money last week," the businessman said to the beggar on the street, "and now you hit me up again!"

"I know it seems I'm ungrateful, but it is just that my federal anti-poverty grant is contingent on my ability to get matching funds out of the private sector!"

✳ ✳ ✳ ✳ ✳

Employer to fired executive: "Oddly enough, I'll be sorry to lose you. You've been like a son to me: insolent, surly, unappreciative."

✳ ✳ ✳ ✳ ✳

As they left the president's office, one executive remarked: "He calls it delegating authority–I call it passing the buck!"

✳ ✳ ✳ ✳ ✳

Boss to his executive assistant: "Rogers, do you have to concentrate all your imagination, initiative, and know-how into your expense account?"

"HOW ABOUT IF BUSINESS PICKS UP, SIR?"
WILL WE GET OUR CORPORATE JET BACK
THEN?"

Boss to tardy office boy: "Instead of a gold watch in 50 years when you retire, we've decided to give you an alarm clock *now*."

✳ ✳ ✳ ✳ ✳

An employment office was checking on an applicant's list of references. "How long did this man work for you?" a former employer was asked.

"About two weeks," was the quick reply.

"He told us he'd been with you a long time," said the caller.

"Yes, Sir," answered the ex-employer, "he'd been here two years."

✳ ✳ ✳ ✳ ✳

Employer to beautiful blonde who has filled out a job application: "Miss Brown, under 'Experience' could you be a little more specific than just 'Wow'?"

✳ ✳ ✳ ✳ ✳

From the *Los Angeles Times*: "Large manufacturing plant has excellent opportunity for assistant office manager. This is not an executive position; job entails considerable work."

✳ ✳ ✳ ✳ ✳

Want ad in *Chicago Daily News*: "Executive Director, from 25 to 40. To sit at desk from 9 to 5 and watch other people work. Must be willing to play golf every other afternoon. Salary over $1,000 a week to start. WE DON'T HAVE THIS JOB! WE JUST THOUGHT WE'D LIKE TO SEE IN PRINT WHAT EVERYONE IS APPLYING FOR."

✳ ✳ ✳ ✳ ✳

At a business convention, four executives met after work and began to let their hair down. They decided to talk about their weaknesses with no holds barred. The vice-president of one company agreed to talk first. "Everyone considers me a teetotaler," he began, "but I'm not. Every so often, maybe once a month, I go to another town, get a hotel room, make a night of it all by myself, then come home."

Another executive announced that his weakness was women. "In a strange town, I'll search out an older, discreet woman and spend the night with her, then come home."

"Well," said the third executive, "my weakness is gambling. The horses, you know. Not excessively, but regularly."

Then all three looked at the fourth guy. "Well?" they urged him on.

"It's like this," he said, "very embarrassed. "I love gossip. And I just can't wait to get out of this room and out where I can indulge my weakness!"

✳ ✳ ✳ ✳ ✳

They tell the story of John D. Rockefeller and how he helped a friend collect a large personal debt. It seems his friend complained that he had loaned a business acquaintance $100,000 and the man had never repaid him.

"My suggestion to you is that you sue him," said Rockefeller.

"I can't, dammit," his friend said. "I failed to have him sign for the loan."

"Well, just drop him a line and demand that he pay you the $200,000 he owes you," the oil tycoon explained.

"But he owes me only $100,000!"

"Exactly," said Rockefeller, "and he'll tell you that in the return note he'll write you. *Then* you'll have all the evidence you need!"

✳ ✳ ✳ ✳ ✳

Whispered at the water cooler: "His pride's a bit hurt. He had to ride tourist in the company plane."

✳ ✳ ✳ ✳ ✳

A loan officer remarked to his disappointed customer: "It is one of life's minor disappointments, Sir, to find out suddenly that the man who writes the bank's advertising has nothing to do with the one who makes the loans."

My stockbroker put me into a ground floor opportunity, and from there it was truly easy to go into a hole.

* * * * *

"I want six of my creditors for pallbearers," declared the store owner. "They've carried me so long, they may as well finish the job."

* * * * *

A bank teller stole fifty thousand dollars from the bank and then stole a car and ran off with the bank president's wife. The town had a tough time finding someone else to teach his Sunday School class!

* * * * *

It is a study in contradiction when you consider that the most honest man this country ever had, George Washington, has the banks closing on his birthday. What are they afraid of?

* * * * *

Horace Rumpole was a banker for thirty years. Then he retired. A federal judge did it!

* * * * *

Some banks show amazing ingenuity. This one built a branch next door to a cemetery. And that wasn't all. . .they put up a sign that read: "YOU CAN'T TAKE IT WITH YOU WHEN YOU DEPART THIS EARTH. BUT YOU CAN SURE SLEEP NEAR IT!"

* * * * *

The Saga of AT&T

It was many and many a year ago,
    In the land of the brave and the free,
That a firm did arise and soon grew to great size,

And its name was AT&T;
But its foes cried, "Unfair! You can't hog the whole share!
 A monopoly's bad as can be!"
And they fought very tough and in time, sure enough,
 They were breaking up AT&T.

Thus began a great war like no battle before,
 With a dozen firms running amok;
On came Sprint, MCI, sev'ral more shooting high
 For a slice of the long-distance buck;
And they snow you with ads pushing trendy, new fads,
 Like no hustle you ever did see;
Till you fall for their pitch and you're making the switch,
 Waving bye-bye to AT&T.

Soon you're making a call to a guy in St. Paul,
 When you're hearing a horrible screech;
So you ring him once more and are reaching a store
 Selling kitchen supplies in Palm Beach;
So you're trying again and are getting through when
 You discover your line has gone dead;
And you're fit to be tied, which is when you decide
 That you'll write him a letter instead.

Once a month you get ill from a 14-page bill
 Full of charges you can't comprehend,
Plus a plan ultra-new, bringing savings to you
 Just so long as more money you spend;
Everywhere that you look, there's more gobbledygook
 As they tout Fiber Optics and such,
And you're cursing your luck and you feel like a schmuck
 While your dollars they reach out and clutch.

Yes, they're making a haul when a Talk Line you call,
 And you're ripped off at two bucks a pop;
Check the bundle you've blown for that self-destruct phone
 You bought "cheap" in some ding-a-ling shop;
See that pile on the floor full of phone books galore
 That not even a pack rat would save;
When you're done, put your ear to the ground and you'll
 hear Mister Bell turning 'round in his grave.

Now we're told all the time, it's a terrible crime

When some giant monopoly rules;
"Competition's the way," the economists say,
   Which is what we are taught in our schools;
But from seeing the mess screwing up the U.S.,
   Any imbecile plainly can see
Life was better back then in those ancient days when
   We were screwed just by AT&T.

Pitiless Parodies and Other Outrageous Verse
by Frank Jacobs
Dover Publishing, Mineola, NY: 1994

✳ ✳ ✳ ✳ ✳

Poets for Hire
Henry Wadsworth Longfellow as a Used Car Dealer

Under the sign that says, "Great Buy!"
   The Buick Regal stands;
Two thousand dollars is the price
   This gorgeous car commands
(In truth, I'd take one-fourth of that
   To get it off my hands).

I drove it and the ride was smooth
   (Except for when it stalled);
The engine's good for many years
   (If it were overhauled);
It's like you're in a car that's new
   (And should have been recalled).

It costs a small amount to run
   (If you can get free gas);
It's peppy and has speed to spare
   (Unless you want to pass);
On roads, it handles like a dream
   (If you've been smoking grass).

The seats will give you room to spare
   (And also ailments spinal);

You'll like the ultra-leather look
(Another term for vinyl);
So drive this beauty home today
(Bring cash; all sales are final).

Pitiless Parodies and Other Outrageous Verse
by Frank Jacobs
Dover Publishing, Mineola, NY: 1994

* * * * *

In Saudi Arabia. . .Humpty Dumpty

Humpty Dumpty drilled a new well;
Humpty Dumpty leased it to Shell;
He's now worth a billion, this fortunate gent,
And entertains friends in his 20-room tent.

Humpty Dumpty lives like a king;
Humpty Dumpty knows a good thing;
And that's why each day he is thanking his stars
For people still driving those gas-guzzling cars.

Pitiless Parodies and Other Outrageous Verse
by Frank Jacobs
Dover Publishing, Mineola, NY: 1994

* * * * *

In France. . .Mary Had a Small Cafe

Mary had a small cafe;
The meals she served were nice;
And ev'ryone who came agreed
She charged a modest price.

Mary's prices now are high;
How come? Well, here's the reason–
Today officially begins
A brand-new tourist season.

Pitiless Parodies and Other Outrageous Verse
by Frank Jacobs
Dover Publishing, Mineola, NY: 1994

THE MODISTE

What Dame do Men esteem the least?
The Inexpressible Modiste
Who designates each Foolish Fashion
That Faddists make their Transient Passion.
'Tis she bids Ladies dress in droll
Green boots that lace along the Sole,
Abbreviated Skirts with Gaiters
That greatly edify Spectators,
Or Evening Gowns devoid of sleeves
And otherwise resembling Eve's.
And Women slavishly obey her.
What's stranger still, they sometimes pay her!

The Mirthful Lyre by Arthur Guiterman
Harper & Brothers Publishers, New York & London: 1918.

"We really should find an excuse for staying here half the afternoon. How would you feel about a merger?"

THE BANKER

The Job for which I never hanker
Is that of him they call a Banker,
Who gets cartooned in Silk Top-hats,
White Whiskers, Waistcoats, Shirts, and Spats;
Who perspicaciously arranges
Some Mysteries yclept "Exchanges"
And "Arbitrage" and "Drafts," and lends
Your Cash and mine to Business Friends.
To sit like him and 'tend to Banking,
With all that Money clinking-clanking,
Would try, I'm sure, the Man of Uz,-
"What is it that a Banker *does?*"

The Mirthful Lyre by Arthur Guiterman
Harper & Brothers Publishers, New York & London: 1918

✳ ✳ ✳ ✳ ✳

THE EDITOR

Don't edit Magazine or Journal,
Not even if they call you "Colonel."
The Editor is born for Woe.
(I've been the Thing and hence I know.)
With Open Ears to all Advisers-
Subscribers, Owners, Advertisers-
He toils within his gloomy Haunts
A-guessing What the Public Wants,
Repelling Lovely Authoresses
Who will not Guess the Way he Guesses-
And has to read what every Bore
Has got to say about the War.

The Mirthful Lyre by Arthur Guiterman
Harper & Brothers Publishers, New York & London: 1918

✳ ✳ ✳ ✳ ✳

PUSH-CARTS

Push-Carts, hand-carts, heaped with ends and orts,
    Dodging under motor-truck, dray, and market van-
They are pompous galleons that sail for stated ports,
    You are furtive caravels that trade where best you can.

They are mighty merchantmen that bowl before the breeze,
  Bound for humming harbor towns where bales are
    bought and sold;
You're the little pinnacles that rove uncharted seas,
  Bartering with savages for emeralds and gold.

Push-carts, hard-carts, lined along the curbs,
  Bargaining and chaffering, what have you to sell?
Oranges and cabbages and aromatic herbs,
  Fennel, spinach, celery, and artichokes as well;

Calicoes and handkerchiefs, slippers, toys, and tins,
  Bedding, books, and cooking-pots, hats and chinaware,
Music-sheets and jewelry, stockings, ties, and pins,
  Laces for the maiden's throat and ribbons for her hair!

Push-carts, hand-carts, slowly trundling home,
  Tell me who your captains are–captains, aye, and crews?
Lively sons of Attica, swarthy sons of Rome,
  Syrians, Armenians, and heavy-bearded Jews–

Offspring of the mariners that said the purple fleets,
  Jostled by the reckless wheel and spattered by the mire,
Hardy-souled adventurers, they cruise the city streets
  Seeking still their heritage, the heritage of Tyre!

The Mirthful Lyre by Arthur Guiterman
Harper & Brothers Publishers, New York & London: 1918

✳ ✳ ✳ ✳ ✳

The world is in lousy shape! Pessimists never had it so
good.

✳ ✳ ✳ ✳ ✳

With most of us, success doesn't go to our heads, it goes
to our mouths.

MEANING BUSINESS

Charge your glasses, be upstanding
Toast the saints whose one concern
Is to see that current prices
Coincide with what you earn.

Industry is such a neat word,
Shrewdly culled from Roget's lists,
No one hopefully will notice
That they mean industrialists.

Patriotic, conscience-stricken,
Choking on the food they eat,
They present a noble image
To the victim in the street.

Pensioners, the weak and spastic,
Gaunt in rat-infested holes,
Robbed from birth of health and reason,
Trouble their immortal souls.

They are pledged to honest trading,
Hardly ever to defraud,
While their boundless love of country,
Prompts them to invest abroad.

Leave them to the job they're bred for,
Give these heroes half a chance,
And you'll see the Venus fly-trap
Flourishing among their plants.
Roger Woods

❋ ❋ ❋ ❋ ❋

Real estate developer: An imaginative businessman who makes mountains into. . .what else. . .mall-hills.

❋ ❋ ❋ ❋ ❋

HOW'S BUSINESS?
Here are some likely responses to the above question by various tradesmen.

| SAID THE SAILOR: | Knot bad. |
| SAID THE COFFEE SALESMAN: | It's a grind. |

SAID THE DRUMMER:	It's hard to beat.
SAID THE ASTRONOMER:	Things are looking up.
SAID THE DRESSMAKER:	Just sew-sew.
SAID THE DEMOLITION WORKER:	Smashing!
SAID THE STREETCLEANER:	Things are picking up.
SAID THE PIANIST:	Right on key.
SAID THE BULLFIGHTER:	In the red.
SAID THE GUNSMITH:	Booming!
SAID THE BOTANIST:	Everything's coming up roses.
SAID THE BARTENDER:	It's been pretty tight lately.
SAID THE LOCKSMITH:	Everything's opening up.
SAID THE SEWER WORKER:	I've been getting to the bottom of things.
SAID THE MUSICIAN:	Nothing of note has been happening.
SAID THE COUNTERMAN:	Pretty crummy.
SAID THE COUNTERFEITER:	We're forging on.
SAID THE ICEMAN:	Not so hot.
SAID THE GRAVEDIGGER:	Monumental!
SAID THE TEACHER:	My work is classy.
SAID THE ZOOKEEPER:	It's beastly!
SAID THE FLOOR WAXER:	Going smoothly.
SAID THE DAIRY FARMER:	Cheesy, in a whey.
SAID THE TOBACCONIST:	It's a drag.
SAID THE BAKER:	I've been making a lot of dough lately.
SAID THE TREE SURGEON:	I've some shady deals going.
SAID THE PILOT:	Pretty much up in the air.
SAID THE PHOTOGRAPHER:	Everything is clicking and developing well.
SAID THE DEEP-SEA DIVER:	I'm about to go under.

A Pleasury of Witticisms and Word Play
by Anthony B. Lake.
Bramhall House Publishers, New York: 1975

136 Wilhelm Strasse
Hamburg, Germany
American Zone

Andrews Coffee Company
435 West 139th Street
New York, New York, U.S.A.

Schentlemens:

Der last two schippmundts of koffee ve gott from you vas mitt ratt schidt germixed. Der koffee may be gootenfuff, but der ratt schidt schpoils der trade ve got.

Ve did not see der ratt schidt in der samples vich you sendt befor to us. It iss taken too much time to pik der ratt schidt from der koffee oudt.

Ve order from you der kleen koffee, und you shipt germixed mitt ratt schidt yet. Idt is a mishtake. Yes, No?

Ve like you to schipp der koffee in vun sack und der ratt schidt in vun odder sack, den ve germix to zoot our kustomer.

Vont you bleeze wride if ve should schipp back der schidt und keep der koffee, or keep der schidt und schipp back der koffee. Or do you vant ve should schipp bak der hole schidten vorks.

Ve vant to do vat iss ridt in dis madder, but ve do not lik dis dam ratt schidten businesses.

Mitt Mutsch Respecht,

Hans Bruder
Importer

Pee Ess – Is der price der same as mittout, as mitt der ratt schidt?

Work Hard and You Shall Be Rewarded
by Alan Dundes and Carl R. Pagter
Reprinted with permission of: Wayne State University Press, Detroit, MI 48201-1309

✳ ✳ ✳ ✳ ✳

An elaborate way of characterizing one's boss is by using the following anatomical debate. Curiously enough, this text seems to have a long history. It is almost certainly related to the classical tale of the debate between the belly and other body parts in which the relative usefulness of each part is argued. If this is so, then the office copier in this instance has not created new folklore, but simply provided a new outlet for an old form.

The Boss
When God made man there was only one. The various parts argued about who would be boss. The *hands* said they should be boss, because they did all the work. The *feet* thought they should be boss, because they took man where he could do the work and get food. The *stomach* thought it should be boss, because it digested the food. The *heart* thought it should be boss, because it pumped the blood that allowed the food to be digested by the stomach. The *brain* said, "I have to send all the signals to get each of you to do your job, therefore I am the boss!" The *asshole* said, "I'll show you who's boss!" So he closed up and wouldn't let anything pass. After a few days, the stomach ached. . .the hands were practically helpless. . .the feet could not carry the body. . .the heart was about ready to stop pumping blood. . .the brain's signals were being ignored.

TO ALL THIS, THERE IS A MORAL: YOU DON'T HAVE TO BE A *BRAIN* TO BE A BOSS. . .JUST AN *ASSHOLE*.

Work Hard and You Shall Be Rewarded
by Alan Dundes and Carl R. Pagter
Reprinted with permission of:
Wayne State University Press,Detroit, MI 48201-1309

✳ ✳ ✳ ✳ ✳

Satisfaction has been defined as a condition as satisfying as an income-tax refund.

✳ ✳ ✳ ✳ ✳

Office Definitions
This list of office definitions collected at a Douglas Aircraft plant in Los Angeles in 1964 illustrates the continuity of this form of office folklore. Most of the terms and transmittal instructions will be appreciated by the occupants of any busy office.

"We will look into it". . .By the time the wheel makes a full turn, we assume you will have forgotten about it, too.

"Expedite". . .To confound confusion with commotion.

"Channels". . .The trail left by inter-office memos.

"Coordinator". . .The guy who has a desk between two expeditors.

"Consultant (or expert)". . .Any ordinary guy with a briefcase, more than 50 miles from home.

"To implement a program". . .Hire more people and expand the office.

"Under consideration". . .Never heard of it.

"A conference". . .A place where conversation is substituted for the dreariness of labor and the loneliness of thought.

"To negotiate". . .To seek a meeting of minds without a knocking together of heads.

"Re-orientation". . .Getting used to working again.

"A clarification". . .To fill in the background with so many details that the foreground goes underground.

"We are making a survey". . .We need more time to think of an answer.

"Note and initial". . .Let's spread the responsibility for this.

"Give us the benefit of your present thinking". . .We'll listen to what you have to say, as long as it doesn't interfere with what we have already decided to do.

"We will advise you in due course". . .If we figure it out, we'll let you know.

"Forwarded for your consideration". . .You hold the bag for a while.

Work Hard and You Shall Be Rewarded
by Alan Dundes and Carl R. Pagter
Reprinted with permission of:
Wayne State University Press, Detroit, MI 48201-1309

✳ ✳ ✳ ✳ ✳

FISCAL FITNESS
To keep your health and business lean
Is easy once you find
They both depend on what you do
To trim your bottom line.

BOSS ART
Executive ability
Is quite an art, it's true;
The art of taking credit for
The work that others do.

CAREER MOVES
Advancement meant that we would move
To new jobs that we found;
But now it's us who's staying home
While jobs are leaving town!

The Best of Snickers by Charles Ghigna
Southern Publisher's Group of Pelham, AL.

✻ ✻ ✻ ✻ ✻

A nasty definition of CORPORATE VICE-PRESIDENT:
A guy who takes the padding out of the shoulders of his
suit and puts it all back in his expense account!

"THAT'S B-O-A-R-D, DUMMY!"

Ed Swanson was walking down the street when he met a client and they stopped to talk. Pretty soon, the client asked, "Tell me, Ed, did you get the check my firm sent you?"

"Sure did. Twice."

"Twice? Really?"

"Yep! Once when you sent it to us and once from the bank."

✳ ✳ ✳ ✳ ✳

If you work faithfully eight hours every day, you may eventually get to be boss and then you can work twelve hours a day.

Robert Frost

✳ ✳ ✳ ✳ ✳

"And how's your business going, Elmer?"

"Mighty fine. Best ever," Elmer replied. "As a result, I sleep like a kid."

"You do?"

"Yep! Just like a baby. I wake up every hour or so and cry!"

✳ ✳ ✳ ✳ ✳

Phil Robinson knocked on the boss's door, entered, and said, "Mr. Reisch, I need a raise, I really and truly must have one. In fact, I went to church on Sunday and prayed for that raise."

"Dammit to hell, Robinson," the boss yelled, "you had no right to go over my head in this matter!"

✳ ✳ ✳ ✳ ✳

The insurance adjuster was making his finishing notes about the warehouse fire and the owner of the place stood beside him, waiting for his judgment. After some time, the owner asked: "Have you figured out the cause of the fire?"

"Yep! Friction!"

"Friction? Explain that, will you. . .I don't understand."

"It's really quite simple," said the adjuster. "Just like so many fires today, this one started with the friction of a million-dollar policy rubbed hard against a half-million-dollar warehouse. Simple, eh?"

A wise man once observed that today a man has it made when his name is in and on everything but the telephone book.

✳ ✳ ✳ ✳ ✳

Tom Jenks took the telephone call, sighed, and hung up.
"Trouble?" his partner asked. "That was quite a sigh."
"Not a good day," Tom replied. "An hour ago my laundry called to tell me they had lost my shirt. This call was from my broker. Same thing!"

✳ ✳ ✳ ✳ ✳

"My rise to the top was through sheer ability and one other quality. . .inheritance."
Malcolm Forbes

✳ ✳ ✳ ✳ ✳

Points of general agreement among managers:
　　1. When you are in charge. . ..ponder.
　　2. When you are in trouble. . ..delegate.
　　3. When in doubt. . ..mumble.
　　　　James H. Boren

✳ ✳ ✳ ✳ ✳

The vain executive was at home making over himself in the bathroom mirror prior to leaving to give his big speech.
"I wonder how many great men there are in the world," he mused.
"One less than you think," said his wife.

✳ ✳ ✳ ✳ ✳

Some entrepreneurs are so lazy that if their ship ever did come in, they wouldn't bother to unload it.

✳ ✳ ✳ ✳ ✳

Monday is the best cure for insomnia.

Our company jokester, the vice president, walked out of the office one evening and onto the street where he saw a women's lib exponent hawking the movement's literature and yelling: "Free Women! Free women!" Our jokester yelled at him, "Wonderful. What's the address?"

✳ ✳ ✳ ✳ ✳

Talk about carrying things to an extreme! Consider this cereal manufacturer, who had for years marketed a popular cereal with the title, "SNAP, CRACKLE AND POP." Well. . .this manufacturer became so affected by the women's lib movement that he heeded his wife's demand and changed the name to "SNAP, CRACKLE AND MA'AM."

✳ ✳ ✳ ✳ ✳

At a business convention, two old friends met.
"Haven't seen you for several years," one friend said. "I understand you've started a new business."
"Yep! Sure did. This time it's a nonprofit corporation. We didn't intend it to be. . ..but it is."

✳ ✳ ✳ ✳ ✳

"How's business? What can I tell you! I started this business on a shoestring but that was the very year everybody began wearing loafers!"

✳ ✳ ✳ ✳ ✳

Plan ahead. . .It wasn't raining when Noah built the ark.

✳ ✳ ✳ ✳ ✳

No matter how much planning you do, it'll never replace dumb luck.

✳ ✳ ✳ ✳ ✳

Use your head! It's the little things that count.

As soon as the rush is over, done, finished, I'm going to have a nervous breakdown. I worked for it, I deserve it, and ain't nobody goin' to deprive me of it!

✳ ✳ ✳ ✳ ✳

We welcome advice and criticism and always rush them through the proper channels (one flush always does it)!

✳ ✳ ✳ ✳ ✳

It is a truism that people who seem to think they know everything are especially aggravating to those of us who do.

✳ ✳ ✳ ✳ ✳

It's amazing the changes that wealth can bring to a man. Before I made my fortune, people said of me that I was impolite. Now they call me eccentric. And back then when I criticized someone, they called me rude. Now they say I'm witty.

✳ ✳ ✳ ✳ ✳

Boss: The one who is early when you are late and late when you are early!

✳ ✳ ✳ ✳ ✳

When a man regularly extols the virtues of hard work, punctuality, frugality and the like, you can be dead certain that he's the employer.

✳ ✳ ✳ ✳ ✳

Tom Arquette handed in a list of his expenses while on a business trip. His boss looked them over, then said,
"I can't approve these, Tommy, but I'll make you an offer for the fiction rights."

✳ ✳ ✳ ✳ ✳

Employer: "What in the hell is this huge item listed in your expense account?"

"That was the cost of my hotel."
"This time, I'll OK it. But don't buy any more hotels!"

* * * * *

"Do you know Charlie Clemens?"
"Sure do. He's the guy who made a fortune in crooked dough, isn't he?"
"What do you mean. . .crooked dough!"
"Oh, I mean. . .well. . .he's a pretzel manufacturer, isn't he?"

* * * * *

Organ Recital

A man called his creditors together and told them,
"I owe you about a million dollars. My assets come to $1,200. You can divvy that up. If that's not good enough, you can just cut me up into small pieces and divide those."
One creditor said, "If we do that, can I have his gall?"

American Legion Magazine. 1969
Reprinted with permission of
Milton Berle's Comedy Software
Box 3605, Beverly Hills, CA 90212

* * * * *

"Is it your practice to give the same speech to every corporation to whom you speak?"
"Yes."
"Doesn't that present a problem when you are asked back?"
"Nope, I've never been asked back."

* * * * *

ODE TO THE ALMIGHTY BUCK
(to a lady who keeps her money in her Bible)

Your Bible, Madam, teems with wealth;
    Within the leaves it floats.
Delightful is the sacred text,
    But heavenly the notes.

Tom and Sally Worden were young and ambitious, and so they asked the boss and his wife to come to their house for dinner. The boss and wife arrived and they were half-way through a delicious dinner when their six-year-old son came in. Daddy introduced the lad to his boss and wife, whereupon the kid asked his dad, "Hey, Pop, does she really wrestle on TV?"

✳ ✳ ✳ ✳ ✳

The main reason why some men succeed and others don't is because the former have so little competition.

✳ ✳ ✳ ✳ ✳

The president of a major U.S. corporation had called a meeting of his board of directors. This time, the chief had a grim, tough look on his face.

"Peter Jenkins, I'll let you have it full-blown. You've been taking my secretary out, right?"

"Yes, I have. But I didn't think you'd mind."

The boss then implicated two other vice-presidents, the chief of sales, the comptroller, and the chief of transportation, accusing each of them of dating his secretary.

Then the boss turned to a new board member, a young man, and accused him.

"Sir," replied the young fellow, "I'm not guilty. I have not taken the young lady on a date."

"Good to hear that," the boss said, smiling. "You are just the one we need. Please go outside and fire her!"

✳ ✳ ✳ ✳ ✳

The wishbone will never replace the backbone.

✳ ✳ ✳ ✳ ✳

I know of one who became a person of large doings because on a day he wore, by accident, the wrong pair of trousers. They sorted very ill with his upper gear; consequently, that day, instead of trotting all about the office as usual, he remained assiduously at his desk with the incongruent pantaloons well hidden. He summoned to him all those from whom he required information, even asking the head of the firm, by telephone, to step in when he next went by. He discovered, by the end of the day, that he had dispatched more business than he usually did in a week; he wasted no time in genial to-and-fro; he strongly impressed valuable customers by not rising from his chair. He remained bashfully until all his colleagues had gone home, and so happened to catch an important long-distance call. He specialized in staying at his desk thereafter. By sitting still, he rose to the top of the tree. It was the sheer hazard of a wrong pair of trousers.

* * * * *

Boss to feet-on-desk clerk:
"I'm going to mix business with pleasure, Gardner. You're fired."

* * * * *

Before my husband and I went on a cruise to celebrate our 50th wedding anniversary, I told his secretary that I wanted this trip to be a complete rest for him. No matter what happened, she was not to write him about it. At our first port, my husband received this letter from his secretary:
"Our first catastrophe happened this morning, but I won't write you about it. . . .."

* * * * *

Returning to his office after lunch, the executive found this memorandum on his desk:
"Your wife called. She wanted to remind you of something which she couldn't remember but thought you would."

* * * * *

Cutting back on advertising is like stopping your watch to save time.

* * * * *

Doing business without advertising is like sneering at somebody in the dark. . .you know what you're doing but nobody else does.

"WE DON'T THINK T. BOONE PICKENS WILL LIKE YOUR ANSWER TO HIS PROPOSAL SIR!"

Many a small thing has been made large by the right kind of advertising.
Mark Twain

※ ※ ※ ※ ※

Don't be so open-minded that your brains spill out.

※ ※ ※ ※ ※

Diplomacy is the knack of saying, "Nice puppy, nice puppy," until you can get hold of a club.

※ ※ ※ ※ ※

A prime rule for businessmen to observe is this: Do not keep both yourself and your business in a liquid condition.

Chicago Mayor Richard Daley (1902-1975) gave this advice on how to take graft safely:
"Don't take a nickel. Just hand them your business card."

* * * * *

An exhausted businessman once made this observation:
"It's amazing how much work you can get done if you don't do anything else."

* * * * *

The boss called an employee into his office and said,
"Jensen, I got to hand it to you. You're an expert at concentrating your entire attention, imagination, initiative, and daring into your expense account."

* * * * *

This is a great country. Here, any stockbroker, insurance salesman, or computer repairman can become our president. . .so long as he doesn't mind a pay cut.

* * * * *

Self-made men are apt tu be a leetle too proud uv the job.
Josh Billings

* * * * *

Success is not always a sure sign of merit, but it iz a fustrate way tu succeed.
Josh Billings

* * * * *

There are people so addicted tu lying that they can't tell the truth without lying.
Josh Billings

* * * * *

The world is full of willing people. Some willing to work and the rest willing to let them.
Robert Frost

The gambling known as business looks with disfavor on the business of gambling.
Ambrose Bierce

* * * * *

After paying half-a-million dollars to his former secretary for her sexual harrassment suit, the executive said:
"I've concluded that the most popular color of justice for women is long green."

* * * * *

Peter Edgar, executive vice-president of his company, noticed that his whiskey bottle kept getting emptier and emptier and so he asked his secretary if she'd been nipping on the stuff.
"Sir, I'm insulted," she replied. "I am of English ancestry known for our honor."
"I'm not concerned with your English, Miss Jones, it's the Scotch that bothers me."

* * * * *

There's a company in Massachusetts with such a bad credit rating that even its money is not accepted.

* * * * *

Bob Seeger had just hired a new secretary and she was beautiful, shapely as all get out and Bob really was pleased. Finally, she said,
"If you really thought I was so great you'd buy me a swell mink."
"Sure, I'll do it. . .but you got to keep the cage clean!"

* * * * *

There's not a thing wrong with nepotism so long as you keep it in the family.

Did you hear the one about the son of the successful businessman? The lad wouldn't work, spent money like crazy and was a total loss to the family. At last the father was on his deathbed and the son, who was impatient to get his inheritance, asked:

"Hey, Pop, where do you want to be buried?"

The father looked up and smiled cynically. "Why don't you surprise me, George?"

✳ ✳ ✳ ✳ ✳

Is it possible to grow a full beard in an executive's waiting room?

✳ ✳ ✳ ✳ ✳

A father was instructing his son on how to be a man in today's world:

"Two things are vital if you want to succeed in business: One is honesty. the other, sagacity."

"What do you mean by honesty?" the boy asked.

"Always and at whatever cost it may be, keep your word."

"And how about sagacity?"

"Never give your word!"

✳ ✳ ✳ ✳ ✳

My boss uses statistics like a drunk uses a lamppost. . .for his support, not illumination.

✳ ✳ ✳ ✳ ✳

Tom Sullivan was a successful manufacturer of sporting goods, but he had overextended himself and now was terribly in debt. So worried was he that he suffered a heart attack and died.

Now in heaven, he approached the heavenly Father as a new resident. He knelt before God, appraising all the elegant surroundings of heaven. . .good walls, platinum floors, bejeweled furniture. He couldn't resist asking:

"Oh, Lord, is all this affluence, this wealth, yours?"

"Of course. Who else?"

"And is it a fact that days, weeks, months, years mean nothing to you?"

"That's exactly right. It's all the same to me."
"Then, dear God, how about lending me a million bucks?"
"Tomorrow."

✳ ✳ ✳ ✳ ✳

"But if you sell those machines at cost. . .how can you make any money in your business?"
"We figure on getting a fair proportion of the repairs!"

✳ ✳ ✳ ✳ ✳

The founder and principal owner of the Bayou Brass Fittings Corporation was on his deathbed with only his daughter in the room. The old man had made millions in the stock market and was known as the richest man in his town.
"Selma, I'm going to die. I know that, but you'll be taken care of."
"Don't talk that way, Daddy. You'll live to be a hundred and twenty."
"No, Selma, God won't have it that way. Why should he wait till I go up to a hundred and twenty when he can get me at eighty-one."

✳ ✳ ✳ ✳ ✳

Did you hear of the small businessman who closed his shop after the first year of business. He hung this sign in his window: OPENED BY MISTAKE.

✳ ✳ ✳ ✳ ✳

Prominent executive that he was, the widow had many visitors offering condolences. Smokers, most of them, put their ashes in the container holding the deceased's ashes, not knowing that his ashes were there.
A month or so after his death, his widow picked up the container and considered it carefully.
"Hmmm," she remarked, "I do think that he's put on a little weight."

✳ ✳ ✳ ✳ ✳

"My boss never gets tired of telling us he's a self-made man."
"Maybe you should tell him that he quit work too soon."

The head of the company, a most unpopular fellow, died and he was on his way to the cemetery with a fleet of cars of his employees following him there. About halfway, there was a gap in the line of the procession and a coal truck pulled into line.

Seeing this, one employee remarked:

"That old boss of ours thought of everything. Why that man anticipated just where he was going and even ordered his own fuel!"

✳ ✳ ✳ ✳ ✳

I'm going to learn to relax even if I have to work at it 24 hours a day, seven days a week.

✳ ✳ ✳ ✳ ✳

Hard work is the yeast that raises the dough.

✳ ✳ ✳ ✳ ✳

A group of successful businessmen were having lunch together. One of them, a huge fellow, mentioned that he'd been on a diet to reduce.

"And I've already lost a few pounds," he said.

"What was the diet?" he was asked.

"One of those high-protein jobs," he replied. "Nothing but steaks and chops. And I'll tell you the truth. In thirty days, I've lost over $250!"

✳ ✳ ✳ ✳ ✳

At the bar where he met his buddies most every night at 5 p.m., Tom Agezio was telling them about his new secretary.

"She's really great," Tom said.

"Does she file your things properly and type fast?" he was asked.

"Not really. She can never find the things I want and she's a real slow typist."

"Then what makes her so great?"

"She also runs real, real slowly."

An executive hired a psychologist to help him select a stenographer. They interviewed forty applicants and narrowed the number down to three. The psychologist met a second day with the three he thought most suitable and asked the first one.

"How much is four and four?" "Eight," she replied.

He asked the second one the same question and heard: "44."

He questioned the last girl with the same question.

"It could be 4 and it could be 44," was the reply.

The three were then dismissed and the psychologist said to the executive:

"The first one gave us a typical example. The second girl certainly showed imagination and the third one was both commonsensical and imaginative. Which one seems best to you?"

"Well, y'know. . .I think I liked that blonde in the tight blouse."

* * * * *

"I'm confident that my secretary is a virgin," her boss said.
"How can you be sure?" he was asked.
"Because she's in the PRIM of life!"

* * * * *

There's a great new drink that all executives adore. It's called a tax cocktail.. Give your date two drinks and she'll withhold nothing.

* * * * *

"DAY OFF"

So you want the day off. Let's take a look at what you are asking for.

There are 365 days per year available for work. There are 52 weeks per year in which you already have two days off per week, leaving 261 days available for work. Since you spend 16 hours each day away from work, you have used up 170 days, leaving only 91 days available. You spend 30 minutes each day on coffee break that accounts for 23 days each year, leaving only 68 days available. With a one hour lunch period each day, you have used up another 46 days, leaving only 22 days available for work. You normally spend 2 days per year on sick leave. This leaves you only 20 days available for work. We are off for 5 holidays per year, so your available working time is down to 15 days. We generously give you 14 days vacation per year which leaves only 1 day available for work and I'll be damned if you're going to take that day off!!!!

Source Unknown

2
SECRETARIES and RECEPTIONISTS

"It's great that they give you a pension in this office. Not only that, but you age a heluva lot quicker here!"

＊ ＊ ＊ ＊ ＊

"I had a funny thing happen this morning," one receptionist said to her husband that night. "I had a phone call and the guy asked, "May I speak to Mr. Enders?" Of course, I asked who was speaking.

The guy replied, "I'm the guy who wants to speak to Mr. Enders."

"And you know what. . .I put him through."

＊ ＊ ＊ ＊ ＊

"I'm just not feeling like myself," the boss's secretary said to him.

"Why?" the boss replied, "that could be an improvement!"

＊ ＊ ＊ ＊ ＊

Cynthia Tobin, Executive Assistant, was amazed to learn that her boss had just purchased a man-eating tiger. The act was so unlike him that she could not resist asking why. "Cynthia, as you know, I recently lost my dear wife. And I've been so lonely that I bought the tiger as a memento to my memory of her."

＊ ＊ ＊ ＊ ＊

My boss loves to joke. When a visitor asks to use our restroom, he says: "Of course. But we only have one so you'll have to take pot luck!"

Clarissa Jones, secretary to the boss, was worried because he was late. Finally, he got there and she inquired whether or not something was wrong. "I just had a big fight with my wife," he explained. "My wife got historical."

"Sir, I think you mean hysterical, don't you?"

"No, I mean historical. Just that. She kept bringing up my past mistakes!"

* * * * *

The boss called his secretary into his office and said, "Your typing has gotten a lot better, Mary. I found only three mistakes. Now type the second word."

* * * * *

Elsie Janis was giggling uncontrollably when she got to the coffee stand.

"What's got into you, Elsie. . .why the hysterical giggles?"

"It's my boss," Elsie managed to gasp. Then she broke into more giggles. Finally she quieted and said, "My boss came in furious today. It seems he went to an artist to have an oil portrait made. When it was finished, he shouted: 'This damn painting doesn't do me justice!'"

And the artist said: "Sir, justice has nothing to do with it. What you need is mercy."

* * * * *

My secretary sure did cure me of having her select gifts for my wife. How? Well, last December, she bought her a red BMW!

* * * * *

My. . .secretary has to be intelligent, well-groomed, personable, and thoroughly trained in karate.

* * * * *

Edith Joshua is stenographer to our company's top boss. And she plays golf with him, too. Her friends (?) at the office say that she wins more games with her pencil than with her golf clubs.

The secretary set out to clean her boss's desk. But she didn't. She took one look at it and decided that she didn't want to upset the ecology!

✳ ✳ ✳ ✳ ✳

A successful man is the one who has a smart wife to tell him what to do and a secretary who then does it.

✳ ✳ ✳ ✳ ✳

Maybe God doesn't need human beings any more what with computers, vending machines, answering machines, dialing machines, etc.

✳ ✳ ✳ ✳ ✳

Her boss was a woman and, after two years of secretarial work with the bossy woman, she was fired. Just before she left, as she was walking out, she turned to her boss and said, "Ma'am, if you ever get married, I'd love to have one of the puppies!" Then she turned and left.

"MISS ABRAMS, I SAID 'HERE'S THE COMPUTER MOUSE'--NOT A REAL MOUSE!"

Finally the boss had to tell his secretary, "Susan, please don't wear those blue jeans to work any more. From the rear, when you are walking, you look like two puppy dogs fighting!"

✳ ✳ ✳ ✳ ✳

Sarah Mae came into the office weeping bitterly, "What's wrong, Sarah Mae?" the boss asked.

"Oh, our divorce just became final and the settlement was awful."

"Well, we split the house." Now she really wept with abandon.

"That's not so bad, Sarah Mae. He got half and you got half, if I understand you right."

"Yes, but he got the inside and I got the outside," moaned Sarah.

✳ ✳ ✳ ✳ ✳

Modern business in a modern society is no place better illustrated than in my office where DIAL-A-PRAYER also has a fax number.

✳ ✳ ✳ ✳ ✳

I hired a stenographer but after a couple of weeks I had to fire her. She was just too dumb! Why, she had to take off her blouse and brassiere to count to two.

✳ ✳ ✳ ✳ ✳

"It's been a terrible day at the office, Dan," Clarissa told her husband. "The derned computers shut down and everybody had to learn to think all over again!"

✳ ✳ ✳ ✳ ✳

The overworked word processor came into her boss's office, stood before his desk, and cleared her throat to ask for a raise. "Sarah Jane," her boss said, "you already make as much as most of our senior executives and they've all got from two to six kids."

"Sir," his stenographer said, "I thought that you paid people for what they did here. . .on the job. . .not what they did at home on their own time."

* * * * *

My new male secretary is so dumb. Why, the subject of the Pied Piper came up and he thought it was a plumber!

* * * * *

Amanda Brown was having coffee with her friend and she was talking about her boss. "He told me that whenever he feels down in the dumps, he buys a new suit. Well, I'd always wondered where he got his clothes!"

* * * * *

My secretary? Of course, she knows her capacity. But the trouble is that she gets drunk before she reaches it.

* * * * *

"Sure, my boss plays golf," his secretary said. "Is he good at it? Well, I don't know for sure. He plays in the low seventies. He won't go out if it gets any colder."

* * * * *

Her boss called Maybelle into his office and said, "Maybelle, where in hell did you get the idea that because I make a pass at you now and then, that you could do just as you please around here?"
She replied" "From my attorney."

* * * * *

It's lonesome at the top. . .but you sure do eat better.

* * * * *

Why do men call a cute steno gal a "pigeon"?
It's because it's short for "callipygian."
Now it may be a word too very, very
So look it up in a regular dictionary.
It might not be there, cause it's hard to spell,
So handle it by writing "fat lass" without the "L".

Emily, a secretary in our office, says that women who want equal rights with men are stupid and have no ambition!

* * * * *

"I've had the same secretary for thirty years," the executive told his friend. "She's perfect in every way except that she gossips something terrible! And she's old, too. That makes her worn out in every part except her tongue!"

* * * * *

My secretary is the most efficient, able one I've ever had. There's only one thing wrong with her and that's her appearance. This morning she came to work looking like an unmade bed!

"SORRY, BUT WE DON'T NEED A LIFE-GUARD FOR OUR SECRETARIAL POOL."

The personnel manager asked: "Are you good, capable at filing?"

"I sure am," replied the pretty girl applicant. "Look at my nails!"

✳ ✳ ✳ ✳ ✳

The boss called to his new secretary to come into his office. "I'm delighted with your work," he told her. "I found only six mistakes."

"I'm so glad you're pleased with me, Sir," she replied.

"Yes. Now let's go to the second line."

✳ ✳ ✳ ✳ ✳

Our office is gung-ho for women's lib. The other day, they circulated an article describing a local robbery at gun point by a "gunperson".

✳ ✳ ✳ ✳ ✳

Last Monday, our secretary observed, "Y'know, I went to church last Sunday and, y'know, after the service, I had the feeling that when God made man, he was only fooling around."

✳ ✳ ✳ ✳ ✳

The boss was furious with the changes his secretary had made in his dictation to her. "I want no changes in my wording. Do you understand that, Miss Brown? Please write my letters just as I give them to you. . .without any changes or additions. Got that?"

The secretary nodded, sat down and began to take dictation.

When she returned with the letter, it read like this: "Dear Mr. Johnes. . .the jerk spells it with an 'h'. Thinks it more aristocratic! His father was a bricklayer. Can you imagine! As to your recent letter, and if you can read his handwriting you deserve an award! You ask what discount we can allow you on 60,000 cans of our vegetable/beef soup. Our very lowest discount is. . .Hey, George, that large chain, JOHNES, wants 60,000 cans of vegetable/beef soup. What discount can we give him? How about 50%? Yeah, I know our best discount is 47% and the most we offer but this guy puts an 'h' in his name so we'll go a little further. OK? Right. So be it. Trusting to receive your order by return mail, etc., etc., etc."

* * * * *

Advice to women in the office: It is OK to appear attractive in your dress, but it is not OK to seem seductive. It is well to dress so as to be attractive yet be dressed for self-defense, too.

* * * * *

Eddie Picatto dictated to his new secretary, a letter to his wife. A short time later, she brought the finished letter to him for signature and the letter was fine except for one omission. .she had not included his final words, "I love you."
"You forgot my last three words to my wife," her boss said.
"No, Sir. I didn't forget. I just didn't realize that you were dictating."

* * * * *

The new secretary walked by and one fellow says to his friend as she passed, "Who said she was all thumbs!"

* * * * *

Two secretaries were having a drink of water and one said to the other: "You know that new efficiency expert they hired? Well, he's had his eye on me too damned often lately. Honestly, I don't know whether to act busy or interested."

* * * * *

Receptionists are really invaluable. They are like those metal detectors you see at the airport!

"I'M WORRIED. MY SECRETARY IS THREATENING TO MOVE OUR RELATIONSHIP FROM THE PRIVATE SECTOR TO THE PUBLIC SECTOR."

Mr. Aarons had had trouble with his last secretary concerning her mathematical accuracy. So with the new girl, he took no chances. "Miss Elmo," he said to her. "You will add every column of figures at least three times before you bring the result to me. Got that?"

"Yes, Sir, I sure do," she replied. Then she left the room to return a half hour later.

"Here are the figures you requested, Sir. And I took even more precautions than you suggested. I added these figures not three but eight times. And here are my eight answers!"

* * * * *

First secretary: "Just look at that new IBM machine we just got. They say it'll replace thirty men."

Second secretary: "Ain't that a cryin' shame!"

Asked if she liked her new stenographic job with the large insurance agency, she replied, "Yes, I like my job a lot. But there is this one guy who is kind of a pain."

"Really?" responded her friend.

"Really! Because he's bigoted."

"In what way is he bigoted?"

"He's got this prejudice that says words can only be spelled one way."

* * * * *

A good secretary can do a whole lot more than take dictation, type, and make coffee. She must also be able to create the illusion that the boss is in charge.

* * * * *

The personnel manager walked into the room and introduced to the head of the department, an extremely mini-skirted new employee: "This is Miss Alders, your new stenographer. She sorts out the men from the boys!"

* * * * *

An auto parts manufacturer was suddenly called out of town and told his new secretary, "I've got to go to the Albert Parts Company for a meeting and I'm supposed to be in Milwaukee that same day for a meeting with Allis-Chalmers. Write and say I've been called out of town to Texas but will phone them when I get back. Sign my name."

When he got back from his meeting with the Albert Parts Company, he found this letter on his desk.

"Alice Chambers
Milwaukee, Wisconsin

Dear Alice Chambers:

I am going out of town to an emergency meeting and can't keep our date."

After he had read the letter, the executive called Allis Chalmers and said to his counterpart there, "I hope you haven't received a certain letter from us."

"Received it! Hell yes, we received it! It's been pinned on the company billboard ever since we got it!"

A very attractive secretary stood talking to a fellow worker, a man, at the coffee table. "Of course, I can tell you how I got my raise," she said to him, "but I'm afraid it won't help you a darned bit!"

* * * * *

An employment office was checking the references given them by a fellow who needed a job. So they called his last place of employment and asked: "Was Mr. Jones a steady worker?"

"Steady, well, I guess!" was the reply, "and more than that, he was so steady he was absolutely motionless!"

* * * * *

The pretty, young stenographer was called back to the office where she'd applied for a job. "Miss Elkins," said the boss, "we think you qualify for this job and offer it to you."

"Gee, thanks, Sir, but I got to tell you this before I accept. "There won't be any opportunities for advances."

* * * * *

The new secretary walked into the office on her first day on the job. She asked the pretty receptionist how to get to Mr. Hartnick's office. "That's easy," the receptionist said. "Just go down that hall until a red-headed guy winks at you, then turn right and keep going until you reach an office where you'll hear, 'WOW!' Turn and go in there. That's your new office."

* * * * *

His secretary is the type who wears mini skirts so danged short that the only thing they don't show is her nationality.

* * * * *

Peter Jennings was dictating a letter to his secretary: "Please head the letter to the firm of Paulson, Edgar and Revers: 'Gentlemen:'"

The secretary broke in and said: "Sir, I think you've headed this letter wrong. I've dated all three of those guys and none of 'em is a gentleman!"

The new secretary was a stunningly beautiful blonde and her boss was the envy of his co-workers. He was disillusioned about her, however, after he dictated a letter to a publisher, told her to sign his name and mail it. For the address, he handed her the publisher's letterhead.

Next morning the mail room returned the letter for lack of sufficient address. The envelope read: "Macmillan Company, New York, London, Tokyo."

✳ ✳ ✳ ✳ ✳

"This new guy we hired is a real dunce," his secretary said to the employment boss. "I think we should rename him."

"Let's call him 'Sanka'. . .because he hasn't an active ingredient in his head!"

✳ ✳ ✳ ✳ ✳

The secretary asked her boss the difference between a recession and a depression. "Let me put it this way," the boss said. "In a recession you merely have to tighten your belt. But in a depression, you ain't got no belt!"

I ALWAYS THINK OF SNOW AS NATURE'S WHITE-OUT.

Being at work on time, every day, is one way to assure your job and. . .that you'll be first to hear most of the gossip.

✳ ✳ ✳ ✳ ✳

A secretary for a vice-president of a major American manufacturing company had worked for the company for just short of a year. Then she was fired.

"Why?" she asked her boss.

"Because for one solid year you've been using the wrong filing cabinets. You've been putting all my incoming and outgoing mail down the wastepaper chute to the furnace, not our filing cabinets.

"Fortunately, although you lost over twenty-five hundred letters, I haven't needed a one of them."

✳ ✳ ✳ ✳ ✳

Mary Ann came into the office one day carrying a cigarette carton. The boss looked at her and said: "Mary Ann, you always complain about not having enough salary and here you are with a box of expensive cigarettes."

"Hey, wait a minute, Sir," Mary Ann responded. "I'm moving and this box holds all my belongings!"

✳ ✳ ✳ ✳ ✳

My boss's secretary is a truly direct, honest person. The other day, a visitor came in to see the boss and his secretary said: "Please tell me. . .would you care to be seated or should I book you into the nearest hotel?"

✳ ✳ ✳ ✳ ✳

The boss called his secretary into his office and told her: "We've got to quit being lovers, Mayrose, because if I spend any more money on you, my wife is sure to find out."

"If you don't spend more money on me," his secretary replied, "I assure you that she'll sure as hell find out!"

My secretary isn't the brightest in the company. The other day she answered the phone and the operator said: "Long distance from New York."

My secretary replied, "It sure is," and hung up!

* * * * *

Most secretaries can manage the office just as well as their boss. And why shouldn't they? They get blamed for what goes wrong anyway.

* * * * *

The secretary has to be as efficient at the business as the boss. Luckily, that's not too hard to do.

* * * * *

Ad in Thompsonville, Connecticut, *Press*: "WANTED–Man to manage Accounting Department in charge of 20 girls. Must like figures."

* * * * *

Doctor: "Frequent water drinking prevents you from becoming stiff in the joints."

Patient: "Yes, but most of the joints don't serve water."

* * * * *

The personnel manager addressed the young man seeking a job, "Tell me," he said, "what have you done?"

"Me?" answered the confused applicant. "About what?"

* * * * *

A woman filling out an application came to the square marked "age." She didn't hesitate. She simply wrote: "Atomic."

* * * * *

Office girl, leaving on vacation, told her substitute: "While I'm gone, you'll go right on with what I was working on–but that doesn't include Mr. Jones."

Glamour girl to male fellow worker: "Sure, I can tell you how I got my raise, but it won't help you much."

✳ ✳ ✳ ✳ ✳

Steno to caller on the phone: "He's out to lunch now, but he won't be gone long–nobody invited him."

✳ ✳ ✳ ✳ ✳

Some secretaries may not be able to add but they certainly can distract.

✳ ✳ ✳ ✳ ✳

One steno complaining to co-worker: "That handsome young executive asked me if I had a date for this evening and when I said 'No', he piled all this work on my desk."

"IF IT'S ONE THING I CAN'T STAND, IT'S SOMEBODY LOOKING OVER MY SHOULDER WHILE I'M TYPING!"

Tardy secretary to boss: "I'm really not late. I took my coffee break before coming in."

✳ ✳ ✳ ✳ ✳

One advantage of a recorder is that they never take a man's mind off his work by crossing their knees.

✳ ✳ ✳ ✳ ✳

There was a certain Manhattan office known for the licentious behavior of the staff. Finally, one secretary got tired of all the goings on. She put the typed message in an envelope and put one envelope on the desk of every man who worked there. The message read: "I'm pregnant." They say that life became almost monastical after that.

✳ ✳ ✳ ✳ ✳

The world needs a lot more love and a lot less paperwork.

"It's my topple system. When it topples over,
I know it's time to file."

From *Nothing Serious - Just A Little Chat With The Boss*
Reprinted by permission of Ann E. Weeks, DNS
Passage Publishing, Inc.
Louisville, KY

Bill Roberts was extolling the merits of his new secretary. "It's not that she types real fast but she can erase thirty words a minute."

* * * * *

A single girl arrived at her office carrying cigars and candy tied in blue ribbons.

"What's the occasion?" asked one of her co-workers.

She waved her hand to show off a sparkling diamond and said, "It's a boy–190 pounds!"

3
SALESMEN and SALES

We're a lot more circumspect today in making our pitch for our products. But we still have our share of con-salesmen like the one (artist?) below who, back in 1851, entertained (and sold) the customer of his day.

An Old-Time Pitchman's Spiel

The itinerant fellows who frequent our village, during the sessions of the Courts, and on all other occasions of popular assembling–vending their small wares, a la the Razor-Strop man–are sometimes very amusing. We noticed one of 'em, last week, crying his *erasive soap* to as simple a crowd as we have observed in some time. He was a sharp-eyed fellow, with a sanctified look, black whiskers, and a still blacker and enormous straw hat.

"Gentlemen," he said, or rather sang–"gentlemen, I offer you a splendid article, a superb article, an incomparable article–magical, radical, tragical article!" [Here he displayed a cake of his soap.] "Magical, radical, tragical, *erasive* soap! Yes, in its effects upon its inventor most tragical! Shall I tell you how? It was invented by a celebrated French chemist, after twenty years of toil, labour and privation. In just fifteen minutes, two seconds and a half after the discovery, he fell into the arms of death, and his name became immortal! You can draw your own conclusions, gentlemen!

"Magical, radical, tragical, e-ra-sive soap! Yes, there's a man has got a cake of the incomparable, inappreciable, infallible, invaluable, magical, radical, tragical, e-ra-sive soap!

"Gentleman, you'd open your eyes, if I were to tell you half the wonders performed by this in-com-pa-rable article.–It cleans oil-spots, removes stains, hides dirt, brightens good colours and obliterates ugly ones!–such is the virtue of the all-healing, never-failing, spot-removing, beauty-restoring, health-giving, magical, radical, tragical, e-ra-sive Soap!" The vender wiped his brow, heaved a sigh, and recommenced, standing at ease against a piazza-post.

"Why, gentlemen, when I first became acquainted with this inextollable gift of divine Providence to erring man, I had an obstruction of the vocal organs, an impediment of speech, that bid fair to destroy the hopes of the fond parents who intended me for the bar or the pulpit. I was *tongue-tied*–but I came across this precious compound-swallowed just half an ounce, and ever since, to the satisfaction of my parents, myself, and an assembled world, I have been volubly, rapidly, and successfully, interminably, unremittingly, most eloquently, sounding the praises of the incomparable, infallible, inimitable, inappreciable, never-failing, all-healing, spot-removing, beauty-restoring, magical, radical, tragical, erasive soap!

"Ah, gentlemen, a world without it would be naught! It takes the stains from your breeches, the spots from your coat, removes the dirt, and diffuses a general cheerfulness over the character of the whole outer man! True, gentlemen, I've worn the forefinger of my right-hand to the first joint, in illustrating the efficacy of this ineffable compound; but I hold that the forefinger of one man–yea, or the forefinger of TEN MEN–are as nothing when compared with the peace and welfare of society and the world!

"Oh, magical Soap! oh, radical Soap! oh, tragical Soap! What wonders thou dost perform! The frightened locomotive leaves its track (*as it were*) on thy approach! The telegraphic wires tremble and are dumb in thy presence!

"Why, gentlemen, it clears the complexion of a Negro, and makes a curly-headed man's hair straight! It removes the stains from the breeches and the spots from your coats–in like manner, it purifies the conscience and brightens the character! If you're a little dishonest or dirty, try it! If your reputation or clothing is a little smutted, I'll warrant it! For ladies whose slips–I mean these little brown, yellow, white, blue, and many-coloured *slippers*–have become soiled, it is the only cure, panacea, medicamentum, vademecum, in all globular creation. Then come up, tumble up, run up, and jump up, like Hung'ry patriots and buy my incomparable, infallible, ineffable, inappreciable, coat-preserving, beauty-restoring, dirt-removing, speech-improving, character-polishing, virtue-imparting, company, ERASIVE Soap!"

Here Hard-Cheek's oratory was interrupted by a shower of dimes from boys, men, and hobble-de-hoys, and the "show" was considered "Closed."

A Treasury of American Folklore
by James S. Tidwell.
Crown Publishers, New York: 1956

A man entered one of the most exclusive men's clothing stores in America. The salesman took him to a private office, seated him, went behind an ornate desk, and asked him about his educational background, father's occupation, religion, and political party. The man, confused, asked why he needed all this information.

"Sir, we just don't sell you a suit. We make you a suit that fits all facets of your life and personality. We buy only imported wool of a type to fit your personality. The wool is processed precisely to fit your way of life. Then we weave the wool in that part of the world where climate and social conditions fit you and your personality. After several fittings, we style a suit to exactly fit you. . .YOU alone. Then. . ."

"Hold on a sec," the customer explained. "I need this suit for a special event day after tomorrow."

"Never worry," the salesman said, "you'll have it."

* * * * *

This new salesman we hired, well, he's the dumbest thing in town. They named a town in Massachusetts for him. .marblehead!

A man brought his dog to a popular evening club and the dog padded right to the piano, seated himself and began to pay some popular songs of the day. The manager of the club was astonished and said to the owner: "Man if you do this thing right, you can make a fortune off that dog. There isn't a theatrical agency in the country that wouldn't bust a gut to have him on their list."

But the owner only nodded and said: "I know all that. But this damned dog's got no sense. He wants to be a doctor!"

✳ ✳ ✳ ✳ ✳

Don't ever tell your client that you'll sell them our product for a song. . .they always ask for the accompaniment.

✳ ✳ ✳ ✳ ✳

The sales manager was lecturing his staff on how to handle a customer who always complained about the prices. "Tell him this story," said the sales manager.

A friend of mine could no longer care for his horse, so he looked around for a place to board the animal. The first place he went asked $30 a day and demanded to keep the manure. That seemed too high, so the man went to another place. They wanted $25 a day. He went to a third boarder of horses and this guy only wanted $10 a day. "And what about the manure?" my friend asked.

"At $10 a day, there won't be any manure," was the reply.

✳ ✳ ✳ ✳ ✳

Definition of an efficiency expert: A man who is smart enough to advise on how to operate your business and far too intelligent to start one of his own.

✳ ✳ ✳ ✳ ✳

Instead of giving us an expense account with which to entertain our customers, they gave us. . .would you believe it. . .a gift certificate to McDonalds.

Jerry Peevy was having a drink at the tavern and sat with some of his buddies commiserating with one of them who had just lost his job. "Money isn't everything," consoled one of the boys.

"I don't know about that," said Jerry, "but I do know this... it beats anything else that comes next."

* * * * *

Be careful when you hear that opportunity comes knocking because it just might damage the door.

* * * * *

"That old house is going to be mighty hard to sell," said Pete Urbankus, the real estate salesman. "Why, when I went through that place I discovered that even the termites were wearing crash helmets!"

* * * * *

"That old building is going to be mighty hard for me to sell," said Mary Brown, number one real estate salesperson in her firm. "It is really old. Why, they had William McKinley graffiti all over the basement walls."

* * * * *

I don't know why I bought that retirement policy from the guy. But I do know that he can retire if I keep up the payments for ten years.

* * * * *

The salesman had just sold a very good fire insurance policy and he asked the buyer: "Do you have any notion of just how much you'd get if your building burned down tomorrow?"

"Yeah, I do," replied the client. "From six to twelve years."

* * * * *

Sales manager to unsuccessful salesman: "I don't know what I'd do without you, George, but I tell you this. . .I'm going to try."

"BOY — WHEN HE GETS MAD, HE YELLS!"

That last salesman of ours sure does speak his mind. The trouble is that habit limits his conversation.

* * * * *

A salesman was describing certain economic conditions to his high school-age son: "When they speak of a recession," he said, "it means that you tighten your belt. When they talk about a depression, that means that you have no belt to tighten. And when you fall into a panic, for sure you have no pants to hold up."

* * * * *

An account executive of a St. Louis stocks and bonds firm telephoned a wealthy matron who had recently purchased her very first-ever shares of stock. Excitedly, he told her that the firm whose stock she'd purchased was going to split.

"My, oh my!" the old lady replied, "ain't that a shame! And they've been together for so very long!"

A man returned to his home in a tropical forest after a visit to the United States. He carried two sets of skis as he entered his hometown. He was asked: "What impressed you most about the United States?"

His answer: "The salesmen."

* * * * *

It is simply amazing to see the persuasive power of some salesmen. I once knew a guy who sold a farmer a milking machine and this farmer had only ONE cow. Not only that, but he took the cow as a down payment. Now *that* is salesmanship!

* * * * *

Did you hear about the salesman who was bald-headed and whose wife seemed never to let up nagging him about it. In fact, she was so persistent a nag about his bald head that it turned gray!

* * * * *

A desperately poor fellow walked into a clothing store and asked the boss for a job. "I really need one," he said. "My family is hungry and we haven't a penny. Can you help me?"

The owner said, "I can't talk to you now. I'm meeting a fellow and I got to go. But take a look at that awful plaid suit over there. If you can sell it by the time I get back, you've got a job."

An hour later, the owner returned and the place looked like a hurricane had struck it. . .clothing scattered everywhere, racks overturned, clothing littered all over the floor. He said to the poor guy he'd given a chance. . ."What the hell happened in here while I was gone?"

"Oh, I had a customer and sold him that plaid suit. He was blind, poor fellow, but that seeing eye dog he had was one tough bastard!"

* * * * *

"You ought to feel honored, Sir. Today, I've had eleven calls and I've refused to see any of 'em." The salesman replied: "I know that, Sir. I'm all twelve of them!"

Sitting next to Reverend Jerald Baskin was an elderly lady who was obviously getting more and more disturbed at the raging storm outside their bumping, sliding airplane.

"Reverend, Sir," she asked tremblingly, "can't you do something about this terrible storm?"

He replied: "Lady, I am in sales. . .not management."

＊ ＊ ＊ ＊ ＊

Today there are sales everywhere. and they make them seem like real bargains, too. I went into a shoe store the other day and asked for a pair of twenty dollar shoes. The salesman brought them out, saying, "Today, these are only twenty dollars a foot."

＊ ＊ ＊ ＊ ＊

Another clever dun for an overdue bill read: "My Dear Sir: It is true that money can't buy happiness. But it can't buy anything else either until you send us the money you owe us."

"WE'RE CONDUCTING A SHOPPER-FLOW STUDY FOR THE NEW GIANT OAKDALE MALL."

A terribly shy-appearing young man walked into the office of a tough, brusque sales manager and said: "Sir, I don't think you want to buy any life insurance today, do you?"

"Hell, no!"

"Just as I thought," said the shy young fellow and started out.

"Come back here, young fellow," demanded the sales manager. "You are the worst damned salesman I have ever seen! You want to inspire confidence, at all costs, and to do that you've got to have confidence in yourself. Got that? And to show you that you CAN make a sale, here's a check for ten thousand dollars for a policy!"

After signing the application that the shy young man presented, the sales manager went on: "You got to master some useful, effective techniques and use 'em!"

"Well, I do just that, Sir," returned the salesman. "I use a different approach for every type of businessman. The one I used on you just now is standard for my approach to sales managers!"

✳ ✳ ✳ ✳ ✳

"How are things going?" the veteran salesman asked the new and green young salesman.

"Lousy!" replied the young man. "Every place I try I get insulted!"

"That's sure odd," the old salesman replied. "I've been at the business of selling for nigh onto fifty years. I've had doors slammed in my face, water dumped on me, been tossed down the stairs, beaten by doorkeepers. . .but insulted? Never!"

✳ ✳ ✳ ✳ ✳

If we could sell experience for what it cost us, we'd all be very rich.

✳ ✳ ✳ ✳ ✳

John Rogers of the Acme Real Estate Agency answered a phone call only to hear a voice ask: "Is this the store that sells maternity clothers?"

John replied: "No ma'am, it's not. But you are going to

need a bigger house, aren't you?"
Now *that's* salesmanship!

* * * * *

After waiting for almost two hours, the salesman walked up to the receptionist and said: "Isn't it just lovely that we can grow old together. . .here in this office!"

* * * * *

That jerk of a securities salesman was so crooked that when he pulled the wool over your eyes, you could be sure it was half polyester!

* * * * *

The sales manager was addressing a meeting of all of her sales representatives: "Gentlemen," she began, "if I were to paint a picture of last year's sales for you, it would be a still life."

* * * * *

"I've got to get a better mix of salesmen," the sales manager told his boss. "When their actual sales figures come up to my projections, you can be sure it is pure coincidence!"

* * * * *

One of life's big mysteries is why they always give a gold watch to the folks who retire to whom time means zilch!

* * * * *

My boss lives in an extremely quiet neighborhood. It seems kind of like a cemetery with lights.

* * * * *

How many applicance salesmen does it take to screw in a light bulb? One and one only, but that is this week and only this week!

The new salesman was on a temporary basis until he proved his sales ability. His first customer was a woman who had just lost her husband and needed a suit in which to bury him. And this new guy sold her a suit. . .with two pair of pants. He kept the job!

* * * * *

Elmer made a lot of money selling insurance. Why, he's so rich that he doesn't bother to empty the ashtrays in his car, he just buys a new one.

* * * * *

An elderly salesman took his wife with him on one of his business trips. They were late arriving in Los Angeles and all hotel rooms were gone except the bridal suite. Offered this last resort, the husband was puzzled and hesitated to take it.

"Is there a problem?" the desk clerk asked.

"Well, we've been married almost forty years and for us to take the bridal suite seems. . .seems. . .well. . ."

The desk clerk said, "Sir, if I were to offer you the ballroom, you wouldn't have to dance in it, you know." (Now THAT'S salesmanship. . .!)

* * * * *

This guy was being overworked and decided to go to the boss for a raise. He said, "Sir, you've got me doing the work of three men. I believe I deserve a raise."

So the boss fired all three of them!

* * * * *

The customer is always right,
The son-of-a-bitch
Is probably rich,
So smile with all your might.
Noel Coward

* * * * *

Don't give the customer what they want–make it better.

Boss at a business meeting: "Do any of you people have any idea of the meaning of a *misleading figure*?"

One man raised his hand, "I do, Sir. It's a woman in a girdle!"

* * * * *

It was a miserable day outside the bar with snow pouring down and high winds causing big drifts. The saleswoman looked through the window at the raging storm, turned to the bartender and said, "Do you think the roads'll be clear enough for me to travel tomorrow?"

"Depends on whether you're on commission or salary, doesn't it?" was the reply.

* * * * *

Pete was having a cup of coffee and reading the newspaper when his buddy, Elmer, came in the coffee shop. "Hey, Pete, how come you aren't at work at this time of day?"

"Oh, I had a heluva argument with my boss and I ain't goin' back to work till he takes back what he said to me."

"What'd he say?"

"You're fired!"

* * * * *

There's no such thing as lousy customers or clients–as long as they pay our bills on time.

* * * * *

There is one ploy Bob Dole could use as the 1996 presidential candidate. He could say that, if elected, he could save a whole lot of his office expenses by qualifying for senior citizen discounts!

* * * * *

Whoever said that the customer is always right must have been a customer.

"Isn't that a strange name for a man who deals in stocks and bonds? A *broker?*"

"It may seem strange to you. But that's what you are when you deal with them!"

* * * * *

The best time to relax is when you don't have time for it.

* * * * *

Of all the things you wear, your expression is the most important.

* * * * *

Things have gotten real tough for my department store chain. We're really cutting back. Take our video department. They've a brand new video titled: *The Five Commandments!* Now *that's* really cutting back!

" IT's OUR NEW SUPER FUEL-EFFICIENT MODEL. "

Did you hear about the superb salesman who invited a cute bimbo to his apartment to see his etchings and, you know what. . .he sold her three of them! Now *that's* salesmanship!

* * * * *

The company sent the customer his twelfth invoice, writing on it just this: "This invoice marks the twelfth that we have sent you. It is now twelve months old!"

The customer returned the invoice, writing on it: "Happy Anniversary!"

* * * * *

With some salesmen, the fact that he doesn't listen to his own conscience is due to the fact that he doesn't accept advice from a total stranger.

* * * * *

She was known as a "tough customer" by all the salesclerks. And she was at the perfume counter to buy something to kill that certain smell. The salesgirl was showing her the most expensive perfume they had, saying: "This perfume is our best, absolutely irresistible and overcomes all male scruples. It's irresistible."

"If it's so damned irresistible," the tough customer said, "how come you're still working here?"

* * * * *

Things were truly tough in our store during the depression. Back in 1935, someone accidentally rang the cash register so we closed the store and had a celebration.

* * * * *

Did you hear about the elderly couple who shuffled into the town's largest department store, went to the president and asked the price of the store. The president, sensing a joke in process said: "Our price is fifty-two million dollars," and grinned. The old man turned to his wife and said: "Honey, please give me the paper bag you took from the closet."

His wife handed him the paper bag and he dumped the contents on a nearby table and began to count the bills. When finished, it came to fifty million dollars and he said: "Darn it, woman, you brought the wrong bag."

✳ ✳ ✳ ✳ ✳

"The bill?" the salesman replies to the boss's inquiry about travel expenses. "That's for my hotel bill while calling on our account."
"Yeah, I know. But in the future, don't buy any more hotels."

✳ ✳ ✳ ✳ ✳

Little Willie lit a rocket
That he found in Papa's pocket;
Next day he told his Uncle Stan –
Papa's now a traveling man.

✳ ✳ ✳ ✳ ✳

Luck always smiles on the ones prepared.

✳ ✳ ✳ ✳ ✳

Talk about great salesmanship. The best around involved a salesman whose wife found strange panties, girdle, and bra in his car. This salesman was so good he made her feel sorry for the girl!

✳ ✳ ✳ ✳ ✳

You never get anyplace if you wait for your ship to come in. Man, you've got to row out and meet it!

✳ ✳ ✳ ✳ ✳

There was once a really able con man who invented a medicine that would allow a man to live two hundred years or more. And he sold the stuff on the street. A passerby was interested and asked his assistant if the seller was really three hundred years old as he claimed to be. "I don't know," said the assistant, "I've only worked for him for a hundred and fifty years."

"IT WAS OWNED BY A LITTLE OL' LADY WHO DIDN'T DRIVE IT. SHE USED A MOTOR SCOOTER ON SUNDAYS."

No sailor ever gets valuable experience and learning from calm waters.

* * * * *

He's lost his dough, he lost his biz
And yet throughout his life,
He took his troubles like a man. . .
He blamed them on his wife.

* * * * *

People will buy what you're selling only if they can buy what you're saying.

* * * * *

The new salesman was being shown around the appliance store by the manager. They stopped before the deep-freeze section. "These particular boxes we buy for $300 and sell for

$295," the manager said.

"But how can you make any money when you sell for less than you buy for?" the new man asked.

"Repairs, man, repairs!" the manager replied.

❊ ❊ ❊ ❊ ❊

Be careful of the man who boasts of being as honest as the day is long. See how he performs after dark.

❊ ❊ ❊ ❊ ❊

Successful selling is something like successful hog calling. . .it isn't so much the noise you make as the tone and appeal of your voice.

❊ ❊ ❊ ❊ ❊

A salesman was traveling in Hong Kong on business and went into a store to make a purchase. He did just that, opened his wallet to extract the money and discovered that somehow, he'd accepted a $16.00 bill. Confused at first, he decided to pass it off on the storekeeper who would never know the difference. So he handed it to the oriental storekeeper, who turned to his cash register, rang it, took out the money and handed the salesman two $8.00 bills!

❊ ❊ ❊ ❊ ❊

I never realized how bad our inflation was until I dropped my wallet on the sidewalk and got arrested for littering!

❊ ❊ ❊ ❊ ❊

Johnny Gleason was our salesman for ten years but finally we had to fire him because he was just too damned stupid to get along in the world. Why, he went to a fortuneteller last year and the woman read his fortune for half price!

❊ ❊ ❊ ❊ ❊

Sales conventions are very important. I learn a lot at them. But there is a universal notion that all sales conventions are nothing but wine, women, and song. Nonsense! I have yet to hear any singing!

It's amazing how one salesman can see calamity in a situation while another sees only good fortune. Consider the case of the two salesmen sent to the wilds of Australia to sell shoes in the outback.

When they got out there, they discovered that the natives did not wear shoes! The first salesman wired the home office: "Leaving tomorrow. No business here. These people don't wear shoes!"

The other salesman wired home saying: "Send plenty of shoes. . .all sizes. . .these people need shoes badly!"

* * * * *

A middle-aged salesman has decided that he reached the age when work is a lot less fun and a lot more work!

* * * * *

Sometimes our minds are so geared to the exceptional that we miss the obvious. Consider the border policeman who was suspicious of a Mexican coming across the border on a bicycle with two sacks of sand strapped to the handlebars. He stopped the man, examined the sacks, and found only sand in them. This happened several times. Then, one night, the policeman walked into a bar in the border town and there sat the guy with the bicycle and sand. He joined him at the bar and after a few drinks, asked: "I want to know just what in hell you are bringing into the country. I know you got something hidden but damned if I know what it is. Be a good guy. Tell me."

"Sure. Bicycles!"

* * * * *

In considering ethical business behavior, consider this case. An antique dealer was browsing at an old store in a small town. He noticed that the cat was sipping milk out of a most valuable bowl. He had to have that bowl! But how to get it without tipping off the proprietor of the store as to the treasure he had? He handled it this way. He said, "My, that's a lovely cat you have. My wife would just love it. Would you sell it to me?"

"Maybe," the storekeeper said.

"How about twenty-five bucks. Would that do it?"

"Sure. The cat is yours."

The antique dealer paid for the cat and then said, "The cat seems to love that bowl. You don't mind if I take it along, do you?"

"Oh, I couldn't let you have that bowl," the storekeeper said. "That's my lucky utensil. Why, since I've been feeding my cats out of that bowl, I've sold twenty cats!"

✳ ✳ ✳ ✳ ✳

The customer walked into the store and up to the cosmetics department. "I'd like a really audacious perfume," she said.

The clerk turned, selected a bottle, and offered it to her. "This perfume you do not use if you are only bluffing."

"I know the ad said no salesman would call- the boss says I'm no saleman!"

This fellow goes into a men's clothing store and buys a silk tie. After the bill of sale is made out and the tie wrapped, the guy says, "Wait a moment. I think I'll trade the tie for a suit of underwear." And he does, then he takes the wrapped underwear and starts to walk out. "Wait a minute," the clerk calls out. "You didn't pay for the underwear."

"Why should I? I traded the tie for it."

"But you didn't pay for the tie."

"Why should I? I didn't take it."

* * * * *

There's a sign in front of an Alabama real estate office that reads: WE HAVE LOTS TO BE THANKFUL FOR.

* * * * *

A furniture store devised a clever letter to appeal to customers who are overdue in their payments and it read: "Dear Sir, We note that you are overdue in your payment to our company. Please note that as of March 1, 1996, we have already carried you longer than your mother did–we have carried you for eighteen months!"

* * * * *

You ask how my business is? I'll tell you. Even the people who don't intend to pay aren't buying!

* * * * *

Some sales executives are never satisfied. They remind me of the story of the guy who was crying in his beer. A friend asked what was wrong and the guy says, "Two weeks ago, my Uncle Edgar died and left me $100,000."

"Great. So what's causing the tears?"

"This week my cousin Selma died and left me $150,000."

"That's even better. You are one lucky gent. So why are you crying?"

"I ain't got no more relatives. So I'll get nothing next week."

The sales manager was complaining to a colleague about one of his salesmen. "George is so forgetful that it's a wonder he can sell anything. I asked him to pick up some sandwiches on his way back from lunch, but I'm not sure he'll even remember to come back."

Just then, the door flew open and in came George. "You'll never guess what happened!" he shouted. "At lunch, I met Fred Brown, the president of a Fortune 500 company. He hadn't bought anything from us in ten years. Well, we got to talking, and he gave me an order with 15 million dollars!"

"See?" said the sales manager. "I told you he'd forget the sandwiches."

Executive Speechwriter Newsletter
American Legion Magazine - 1996
Reprinted with permission of
Milton Berle's Comedy Software
Box 3605, Beverly Hills, CA 90212

* * * * *

Elmer Rankin, the clerk at the tobacco sales counter, was deeply preoccupied with a book and did not notice the customer waiting. Impatient, the customer finally said, "Hey, you with the book, I want some cigars."

"So pick out what you want. I'm busy."

The customer selected the cigars he wanted, put money on the counter, then said: "What in the hell are you reading that keeps you from waiting on me? Must be so-o-ome story!"

"It is. It's a book on salesmanship!"

* * * * *

With banks and stores now advertising their "easy credit" terms, this sign in a store window is a refreshing experience.
Try our simple, easy credit plan:
100 percent down
Not a cent to pay each month!

* * * * *

Buyer: "I hear that fish is brain food."
Salesman: "I know that. I eat it almost every day."
Buyer: "Well, there goes another theory!"

"How's business, Morrie?"
"It's. . .it's looking up. We're flat on our backs!"

∗ ∗ ∗ ∗ ∗

Low Bidders
A man in his beat-up old car drove up to a toll booth. The toll collector said, "Two dollars."
The owner said, "Sold!"

American Legion Magazine - 1996
Reprinted with permission of
Milton Berle's Comedy Software
Box 3605, Beverly Hills, CA 90212

From *Nothing Serious - Just A Little Chat With The Boss*
Reprinted by permission of Ann E. Weeks, DNS
Passage Publishing, Inc. - Louisville, KY

Talk about your tall tales. Well, this one deals with a hair-growing tonic and the salesman who was selling a quart of it to a customer. The customer asked, "Can you promise me that it'll really grow hair for me?"

"I promise. For sure. Evidence? Listen to this. I sold a quart to a customer who bought it for her husband. She took it home, sat him down, pulled the cork out of the bottle with her teeth and within 24 hours, that gal had a mustache!"

* * * * *

One office worker to another: "When Pete retires, how will we know?"

* * * * *

Salesman: "This sewing machine is the best. . .the very best and I promise you that it'll pay for itself in no time."

Customer: "That's just fine. You can send it to me when it does."

* * * * *

Doesn't John Fenn ever run dry?

Once more the Pun Prince of West Palm Beach, FL, John Fenn, unloads tons of puns on us:

I could have been a horse trader but I didn't like the neighborhood.

I could have been a traveling salesman but I had no ware to go.

I could have been a prognosticator but where's the future in that?

I could have been a bank president but I showed a lack of interest.

I could have been a pro golfer but I drove off into the sunset.

I could have been a Velcro salesman but I didn't have the proper connections.

Idioms Delight

Jane lost her job at a dieting center when the office was down-sized.

Jim got his walking papers from the Baby's First Shoes Company.

Tom was canned from the Campbell Soup Company.

When he heard the strange noises in the yard goods store, he bolted out the door.

Pun American Newsletter
Lila Bondy, Editor.   Deerfield, IL 60015

✳ ✳ ✳ ✳ ✳

A perfume salesgirl clinched the sale with: "If he's the sort who can resist this, honey, you wouldn't want him anyway."

✳ ✳ ✳ ✳ ✳

A salesman to a Mae West lookalike. "I represent the Mountain Wool Company, Madam, and I wonder if you'd be interested in some coarse yarns?" And she said, "Tell me a couple."

✳ ✳ ✳ ✳ ✳

We like the bait seller who placed this sign near his house: "Worms with Fish Appeal."

✳ ✳ ✳ ✳ ✳

Sign on department store counter: "Extra-size towels–just what you need when answering the phone."

✳ ✳ ✳ ✳ ✳

Super salesman: Someone who can make you feel that you've always longed for something you've never heard of.

✳ ✳ ✳ ✳ ✳

Saleswoman showing girdle to a very fat woman: "I don't think it will support you in the manner to which you're accustomed."

Two salesmen were driving from one town to another, down a country road, when their car broke down. It was after sunset and they couldn't see to repair the problem. So they walked down the road and came to a farmhouse, knocked on the door and a little old lady opened it. They asked to use the phone. "Of course, come right in," she said.

They called the repairman but he said it was too late. Then they asked the elderly lady if they could stay the night. She said: "Yes, you may. But you'll have to sleep downstairs since I sleep upstairs." They nodded and off to bed they went.

The next morning they had breakfast and walked to the car that they soon had running and were on their way.

Several months later, the one salesman got a phone call from the other salesman. "Do you remember the night we broke down and stayed at that elderly lady's house?" his friend asked.

"Sure do. That was some night!"

"Do you recall wandering around in the dark that night?"

"Yep! Couldn't sleep so I did wander."

"Did you wander upstairs that night?"

"Seems like I did. Yep. For sure I did."

"And did you wander into the old lady's bedroom?"

"Yes, I think I did."

"And did you use my name?"

"Yep! Hope you don't mind that I did."

"Not at all. That old lady died recently and left me the farm and $200,000."

* * * * *

"The two greatest stimulants in the world are youth and debt."
Benjamin Disraeli

* * * * *

"There was one salesman who just never gave up on a prospect. But he was never able to get the job done with the head of a major corporation. He tried and tried to sell the company but never did. That didn't stop him.

Well, at last, this particular executive died and went to his haven of eternal rest. When he got there, he was met by the persistent salesman, hugged, and then invited to see his line. "I'm here for our appointment," he told the executive.

"What appointment?" the executive responded.

"Don't you recall what you said to me time after time? You always said that you'd see me here first!"

＊ ＊ ＊ ＊ ＊

A salesman who specialized in farmland was offering a 240-acre plot to a prospect: "Sir, this is the best land outdoors! All it needs to produce the best crops in the good old U.S.A., is good people and water."

"You don't say," replied the prospect. "But that's all hell needs, too."

＊ ＊ ＊ ＊ ＊

The salesman came in with a long, grim face. "Didn't do much good today," he said to his wife. "I only got two kinds of orders."

Wife: "Oh? What were they?"

Husband: "Get out and stay out!"

＊ ＊ ＊ ＊ ＊

At the flea market, a customer argued the price down and then never paid. "If you didn't intend to buy this, why did you argue so hard to get the price down?"

The customer replied: "I didn't want you should lose too much."

＊ ＊ ＊ ＊ ＊

He was a great salesman. When he worked for a duplicating machine company, he even sold one to a carbon paper manufacturer! Now *that's*. . .salesmanship!

＊ ＊ ＊ ＊ ＊

Here's the way a TV repair shop responded to a customer's check that bounced: "Sir, please come in and see us. We did get the waviness out of your TV set but we can't get the bounce out of your check."

A salesman was offering an appliance to a woman and trying very hard to sell her. "I promise you, Ma'am, that you can pay for this refrigerator with the money you save by using it."

"I know you're right because we're buying our car on the money we save on bus fare, and the same goes for our washing machine–on the money we're saving on laundry bills. And we're paying for our house on the rent money we're saving. But, Sir, we just can't afford to save any more just now."

❄ ❄ ❄ ❄ ❄

Take the humbug out uv the wurld and yu ain't got much left tu do bizzniss with.
Josh Billings

" SCRATCH 3 AND 5. 3'S HAD A FIGHT AND 5'S JUST GOING TO LIVE TOGETHER INSTEAD. "

When Johnny Devere, his company's top salesman, was told they needed to sell another *100* washing machines, he had an idea. He had the machines sent to an old customer and then wrote a letter: "Gentlemen, we are sending you *90* machines at the special price listed on the invoice. A once-in-a-lifetime opportunity for you."

Impatiently, he waited for their check but instead a letter came without a check. It read: "Gentlemen, thanks for the offer, but no. We are returning 90 machines today. Thanks."

* * * * * *

Your creditor has a better memory than you, his debtor.

* * * * * *

Be careful when you say "Laughter is the best medicine." A friend of mine repeated that phrase regularly until his physician sued him for practicing medicine without a license.

* * * * * *

Then there was the guy who was asked: "How's your business?"

He replied: "It's lookin' up. It's flat on it's back!"

* * * * * *

A traveling salesman was forced to stay overnight at a small-town hotel. At 3 P.M., he appeared at the desk announcing that he was checking out.

"What's the matter, Sir? Didn't you sleep well?"

"NO!"

"Something bothering you?"

"Yeah, a dead bedbug between the sheets."

"Don't tell me that a little thing like that would keep you awake!"

"That's exactly what I'm telling you," the salesman said. "All his friends and relatives came to the funeral."

* * * * * *

America is still the land of opportunity. Here a man can start out as a carpenter and end up a contractor. . .if he doesn't mind the loss of income.

For every unexpected order, there are two unexpected cancellations.

* * * * *

How's this for an effective sign advertising a travel agency? PLEASE GO AWAY!

* * * * *

In the dairy department of a supermarket, they posted this sign: We do not claim that milk grows hair, but have you ever SEEN A BALD CAT?

* * * * *

Another supermarket posted this sign in their dairy products department: THE UDDER PLACE.

"I CAN'T DECIDE WHETHER to NAME IT BAGEL, LIFESAVER, OR DONUT."

A shoe salesman had pulled out and shown her every box on the shelves. He flopped down in a chair saying, "Mind if I rest for a few minutes? Your feet are killing me."

✳ ✳ ✳ ✳ ✳

FOUNTAIN-PEN SALESMAN

Now here is a pen that gives you any sort of line without changing the point. Now if you understand, realize, and appreciate a real good value, and if my physiognomy is not too conspicuous to be comprehended, I'm gonna clarify to such an extent that each and every individual standin' here at the present time can very well afford it. I'm gonna give you this Parker 51 type. Now don't forget. You can take my pen and bring it into any pawnshop, ask them for ten dollars, see how quick they'll chase you out. But you ask them for five dollars, they may give it to you. And to-day I'm not gonna charge you no dollar bills for the pens, but the first lady or gentleman gives me twenty-five cents gets the pen. And I think it's worth a quarter to anybody. Any one who understands and realizes and appreciates something real good.

You can go downtown, uptown, out of town, into town, in the summer time, in the winter time, all the way through, you'll never get a pen like this. By golly, that was a heavy quarter. Thank you. Every one gets the same chance. Here is another one like the last one. Look–not to discriminate, to make fish of one and flesh of another–you know. Saturday my wife says to me, "George, I want you to come home. I'm gonna give you something." I have a neighbor that's very nosey–he said to me, "What's she going to give you? What is the wife going to give you? Look at what my wife gave me Friday night. Fish."

Believe me, as long as you live, and may you live as long as you wish, and don't forget that all the money that you spend with me goes to a good cause–'cause my wife wants money–the butcher, the baker–everybody wants money.

Look at this. You can write Yiddish, you can write English, you can print, you can sketch, with this very same pen. You show me another pen, regardless how much you may spend for it, that will give you this service and this satisfaction. Now this being the last demonstration, you don't have to give me no dollar bills. But if you want a pen that makes writing easier for you and yours, a pen that improves your penmanship one hundred and one per cent, here is the pen right here.

Now believe you me, it is very hard to demonstrate, but this is the finest and best. Now every man, every woman, every child who needs a fountain pen shouldn't hesitate one minute in receiving a pen that's superior in quality, in texture, in writing ability, and at a price that can't be beat anywheres. It is by far the finest, the best that money can buy.

Look at the way the pen writes. Here is a pen that slides and glides over your paper just the same as a ball or a marble over a sheet of glass. During this adver-tise-ment, you get this very same pen–*not a dollar and a quarter but a quarter of a dollar*. That's yours. Give me a hundred dollar bill, I'll run away faster than you. Make sure you give me the right amount, because I don't want too much. Four nickels and one is five. God bless your stingy soul!

Everybody who understands what I'm talking about–you know what I'm talking about–you want something that's really good. Why be confused? This is not something that will cure a headache, an earache and a toothache, remove any spots, stains, corns, calluses, ingrowing toe nails–won't make you richer, won't make you poorer. it will do only one thing for you. If you want a pen that will write any language, here is a pen writes English, Yiddish, Chinese, Japanese, Turkish, Scandinavian, upside down, printing, sketching, drawing. Believe you me, when you spend a quarter with me, you find five dollars in the street.

A red one? Right there. You take a green one and it'll turn red. You take a red one and it'll turn green. You have two different colors. Every man and woman who understands–no, I don't care if you're a man that was chased out of the bread line because you wanted to have toast, I don't care if you fell asleep the first night you were married–if that would make any difference–here it is right here. I got a cousin of mine that is the strongest man in the country–he lives out West and he holds up trains.

Believe me, this fellow Milton Berle–there's only one little difference between Milton Berle and myself: he gets a thousand dollars for one song and I get a dollar for a thousand songs. Here is the greatest value you ever anticipated in having in a long while. Now when you see a value of this kind, I guarantee you–look at this–can you show me anywheres a pen as good as this? I think I'll give this one here to the president of the Amalgamated Shoe Stores.

Everybody gets one. Don't hesitate. Hesitation means you'll never get it. First time in the United States of America that you get a value like this. When you go uptown and out of town or anywheres at all, you never see a value like this. Now look at this. . .

Recorded by Tony Schwartz,
West Forty-second Street
between Sixth Avenue and Broadway
New York City, July 1, 1951.
Transcribed by B. A. Botkin

4

TAXES (OH WOE!)
GOVERNMENT (OH WOW!)
BUREAUCRACY (AIN'T NO WHOA!)

APRIL 15TH

Raising Tax is so Alluring
That in Rome they once taxed urine.
If they taxed the same today,
More would willingly, their "Fair Share" pay.
I see citizens in line with anticipatory verve
To give the I.R.S. just what it deserves.

By J.R. Dunn,
Humor & Health Journal,
Vol. 5, No. 2, March/April 1996
Jackson, MS

❅ ❅ ❅ ❅ ❅

Remember the old saying "A fool and his money are soon parted"? Well, that's now a government law.

❅ ❅ ❅ ❅ ❅

In the hills of Arkansas, one redneck told his buddy, "My Uncle Josh wants me to help 'im wid his taxes."
"Is he nuts? Why you can't read or write."
"That don't matter none. All he wants is fer me to pay 'em."

❅ ❅ ❅ ❅ ❅

A businessman was acting as his own attorney in a tax case before a federal judge. The defendant shouted, "As God is judge of my every word, I. . .do. . .not. . .owe. . .this. . .tax. I swear."
The judge responded: "He's not. I am. You do."

"Now, you consider taxes," the boss said to the board of directors. "They are merely another way to say, 'Stick 'em up!'"

＊ ＊ ＊ ＊ ＊

Can you imagine my boss, protesting a decision against him in an IRS case? They disapproved a contribution he claimed to have made to the widow of the unknown soldier.

＊ ＊ ＊ ＊ ＊

It pays to be an American 364 days a year. On that you can bet! But April 15th is the day that YOU pay to be an American.

＊ ＊ ＊ ＊ ＊

April 15th is that one day in the year when you are privileged to pay for the government you've been griping about the rest of the year.

＊ ＊ ＊ ＊ ＊

The only time the average child is as good as gold is on April 15.

＊ ＊ ＊ ＊ ＊

The owner of a small pizzeria in Canton, Ohio was hauled in for an IRS review. It seems that the federal agent had discovered several trips to Europe deducted on the man's income tax return. She asked: "How come you deducted from your tax return six trips to Europe?"

"Oh gosh," the man began to explain, "you see. . .well. . .it so happens. . .in our business to be successful, you have to deliver."

＊ ＊ ＊ ＊ ＊

They say that over the entrance door of the IRS office in Duluth, MN, there's a sign that reads: WATCH YOUR STEP, and as you come out of the building, the exit door has this sign: WATCH YOUR LANGUAGE!

A businessman once asked an Internal Revenue agent if birth control pills were deductible. The agent's reply was: "Only if they don't work!"

* * * * *

When the businessman sat down at the desk of the IRS agent for a review of his tax return, the agent said, "Sir, this income tax return of yours totally blew out all the circuits in our computer!"

* * * * *

It seems that today the whole earth revolves on its taxes.

* * * * *

It is a fact that in America it takes more brains and know-how to make out the income tax form than to make a success!

It is strange that in today's world, which they say is getting smaller, postal rates keep rising.

＊ ＊ ＊ ＊ ＊

A taxpayer is a person who doesn't have to take a civil service exam in order to work for the government.

＊ ＊ ＊ ＊ ＊

When you strike it rich and your ship comes in, well, the IRS will be there to help you unload it.

＊ ＊ ＊ ＊ ＊

Five ways a Federal department might handle the need to replace a burned-out lightbulb:

First way: A supervisor to spot the burned-out bulb, his boss to grant permission to seek a requisition, then a requisition typist with twelve clerks to file those requisition copies, then a clerk to deliver the copies to the purchasing department, an agent to order the bulb, a receiving clerk to receive the bulb.

Second way: One employee to screw it in and another to screw it up.

Way number three: "Never mind about it. We get bids on a contract for such things."

Way number four: Only one but that one'll need two outside consultants to bring it all to a conclusion.

Way number five: One who can assure us that all possible is being done to end the emergency and two others to screw the bulb into the drinking fountain faucet.

＊ ＊ ＊ ＊ ＊

Professional tax planners can save citizens time. And those with tax shelters might save as much as ten years.

＊ ＊ ＊ ＊ ＊

It takes creativity to fill out your tax return. But when you explain that tax return to the IRS, well, that takes plenty of innovation.

It is certain proof that it is truly possible to get badly wounded by a blank. . .consider your tax form!

✳ ✳ ✳ ✳ ✳

It was Patrick Henry who thought that taxation without representation was pure tyranny. One wonders what he'd think of it today when we *do* have that representation!

✳ ✳ ✳ ✳ ✳

Be glad you've got all that government today. Just imagine what it'd be like if we got all the government we've been paying for.

✳ ✳ ✳ ✳ ✳

Being in business today is a no-win proposition: If you do something wrong, you get fined and if you do it right, you get taxed!

✳ ✳ ✳ ✳ ✳

If you think politics is strange, consider how old it is. Voltaire, the French philosopher, said in the 18th century, "In general, the art of government consists in taking as much money as possible from one part of the citizens to give to the other."

✳ ✳ ✳ ✳ ✳

Bureaucracy is a crippling arrangement. If the ancient Egyptians had been saddled with our kind of bureaucracy, they'd still be trying to finish those pyramids!

✳ ✳ ✳ ✳ ✳

A fair description of our Congress is that it is an institution of government where a person rises to speak and says nothing while nobody listens. Then everybody disagrees!

✳ ✳ ✳ ✳ ✳

Isn't it odd how Congress louses things up when they cut the budget? The knife always slips and taxpayers start bleeding.

"NATURALLY, WE EXPECT GREATER TAX RETURNS FROM YOU FOR ALL THE BUSINESS COMING YOUR WAY"

Noah must have taken into the ark two taxes. . .one male and one female, and haven't they multiplied bountifully!
Will Rogers

* * * * *

I'm different from most Americans. I pay my taxes with a smile. But then the government keeps asking for money!

* * * * *

April 15th is the day described as being the one that changes the American eagle into a vulture.

* * * * *

Here's one way of looking at taxes to ease them. Taxes are money and you know that when you die, you can't take money with you. Right? So government is merely being efficient and relieving you of that final decision.

Someone in our office keeps saying the IRS is like a bad, careless laundry where you keep losing your shirt.

* * * * *

A Toledo, Ohio businessman complained that he had always expected to leave his business to his children. But not any more. The IRS beat them to it.

* * * * *

The head of our company is a very charitable man. He told the IRS he had given half-a-million dollars to his church. Well, the IRS decided to check that one out, went to the minister of his church and asked if his parishioner had actually given the church half-a-million dollars. "He most certainly will," the preacher responded.

* * * * *

The boss's secretary thinks that "damn" and "taxes" are one word.

* * * * *

To sell something, tell a woman it's a bargain. Tell a man it's deductible.
> Earl Wilson

* * * * *

Income-tax expert: Someone whose fee is the amount he saves the company making out its taxes.

* * * * *

Conscience is that still small voice that tells you the government might check your tax return.

* * * * *

Mark Twain posed this question, "What is the difference between a taxidermist and a tax collector?"
The answer: The taxidermist takes only your skin!

The income tax has made liars out of more people than...
golf!

✳ ✳ ✳ ✳ ✳

The caller announced to the secretary to the president of the corporation that he'd like to talk with him. The secretary rose, went to the boss's office door, opened it and said, "Sir, the man from the IRS is here."
"All right," the boss replied. "Give him a chair."
"Should I also give him my desk, computer, and file cabinets,too?" she asked.

✳ ✳ ✳ ✳ ✳

April 15th is the best day to count your blessings, after which... you send them to Washington.

INTERNAL
REVENUE
SERVICE

It's gotten so that what were once two words - "damn" and "taxes" are now frequently heard as one.

※ ※ ※ ※ ※

The guy sat down alongside the desk of the IRS examiner who put the man's papers on the desk, turned to his client only to discover that the man was shaking. "Don't be nervous, Sir. This is a simple examination done only to be sure we understand your return." But the client was shaking even harder, so the examiner asked, "Sir, we have hot coffee ready. Would you like a cup?"

"G-g-good," the client stammered. "Please."

The examiner went to the coffee table and poured a cup only three-fourths full, not wanting it spilled when in the hands of the shaking client.

The client took a sip, sighed and sat back, now ready for the questions..

"Sir," the examiner began. "What is your profession?"

"I'm a brain surgeon," replied the client!

※ ※ ※ ※ ※

You might as well count your blessings because after April 15th, you'll have little else to count.

※ ※ ※ ※ ※

Just before April 15, the Internal Revenue Service received a $200 check with this note: "I did not give you the truth on last year's income tax form and my ulcers have been bothering me ever since. Please accept the enclosed check."

Sincerely,
A Repentant

P.S. If my ulcers still bother me, I'll send you a check for the rest of the money I owe.

※ ※ ※ ※ ※

The taxpayer: That's someone who works for the federal government but doesn't have to take a civil service exam.
Ronald Reagan

Guys come up with the strangest ways to avoid paying income tax. This one business refused to pay the government because the tax forms were Greek to its accountants and the boss refused to pay taxes to a foreign government.

* * * * *

It's easy to understand why most businesses feel, after April 15, that the government just flushed their profit!

* * * * *

Tax time is that annual period when our government of the people, by the people and for the people sticks it to the people!

* * * * *

You get fined for doing wrong. You get taxed for doing well!

* * * * *

Two guys were discussing a young lady whom both knew. "She's not so good to look at," one said.
"No, she's not," replied the other. "If her face is her fortune, one thing is sure. . .she'll never have to pay income tax!"

* * * * *

"This is too difficult for a mathematician. It takes a philosopher," Albert Einstein remarked after completing his income tax return.

* * * * *

Here comes Mr. Winter, Collector of Taxes, to suggest you give whatever he asks, and that, with no nonsense or flummery for though his name's Winter, his actions are summary.

* * * * *

To be considerate of the birds, feed them often. The dove brings peace and the stork brings us tax exemptions.

144

Elmer Jorgensen was a prolific author of more than seven successful novels. His fiction was recognized as some of the best published in the United States. When income tax time came around, Elmer took his necessary materials to a professional for completion.

After all work had been accomplished in the professional's office, the latter pushed Elmer's material aside and turned to ask him: "Mr. Jorgensen, which of your several books do you consider to be your best work of fiction?"

"It's in the hands of the publisher now. . .YOU," he said, pointing to his own income tax return papers.

✳ ✳ ✳ ✳ ✳

Did you hear about the audit of a delicatessen owner's income tax? Well, as it turned out, the return wasn't kosher.

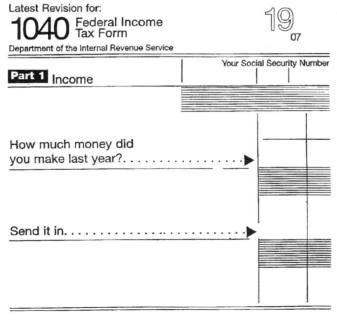

Simplified 1040

Latest Revision for:

1040 Federal Income Tax Form

Department of the Internal Revenue Service

19 07

Part 1 Income

Your Social Security Number

How much money did you make last year?. . . . . ▶

Send it in. . . . . ▶

From *Nothing Serious - Just A Little Chat With The Boss*
Reprinted by permission of Ann E. Weeks, DNS
Passage Publishing, Inc. - Louisville, KY

Three prominent businessmen were having lunch in a fancy Manhattan restaurant and it was now time to pay the bill. The waiter presented the astronomical figure to the gentlemen and one man grabbed it, saying: "I'm in the 50% tax bracket, fellows, so let me pay as it'll only cost me half."

* * * * *

In the presidential election of 1996, I voted for change. Why? Well, that's about all I had left after paying my income taxes.

* * * * *

Did you hear about the guy who went into a bar and the guy had an alligator on a leash? The guy says: "Do you serve IRS agents here?"
"We sure do," said the bartender. "What'll you have?"
"Oh, I'll have a beer. The alligator'll have an IRS agent."

* * * * *

It has been suggested that taxpayers, as a group, adopt a special song to express their feelings. The title: EVERYTHING I HAVE IS YOURS.

* * * * *

We call that special November day, THANKSGIVING DAY. Why not do the same for April 15: TAXGIVING DAY!

* * * * *

"Don't let April 15 bother you, buddy. I always pay my taxes with a smile."
"Man, you're lucky! I have to pay mine with money!"

* * * * *

Johnny Good turned to his wife with a distressed look on his face. "Mary," he said, "I'm really, really worried. Here it is April 16 and I've still got $150 in the bank."

If you are looking for a sure, unchallengable tax deduction, try unemployment!

✻ ✻ ✻ ✻ ✻

That income tax form just about has me buffaloed. I've worked for hours to figure what it is they want me to do. I tell you. . .it takes more brains to figure out that tax form than it does to make the money they're taxing.

✻ ✻ ✻ ✻ ✻

Why isn't the IRS polite and nice like most other businesses! I mean, why don't they say, "If you're not completely satisfied, we'll refund your money."

✻ ✻ ✻ ✻ ✻

We used to say disparagingly, "Success has gone to his head!" Now the phrase has been changed to read that it goes to the IRS.

✻ ✻ ✻ ✻ ✻

"That Pete Jenkins is worth a lot of money," said one guy to another.
"That's what I hear," said his friend. "I heard he had simply untold wealth."
"That's exactly right. And that's the reason the IRS put him in jail."

✻ ✻ ✻ ✻ ✻

The IRS is contemplating establishing an express lane for taxpayers with five loopholes or less.

✻ ✻ ✻ ✻ ✻

A fellow ran into the Post Office in his town and yelled, "I'm being pestered and threatened by somebody writing menacing letters to me. Can you help me?"
"I certainly can," said the town's postmaster. "That kind of letter is a federal offense punishable by a prison sentence. Have you any idea who wrote it?"
"You bet I do. It's those damn income tax people!"

Boy, was I mad! I went to the IRS office, stormed through the door and up to the agent and really let him have it! Every last penny I had in the world!

✳ ✳ ✳ ✳ ✳

In Pasfield Park, a motorist heard a woman screaming for help. He stopped the car and rushed to her. "Oh, Sir, my little boy just swallowed a quarter and he's choking. Can you help?"

The fellow picked up the boy by his ankles, turned him upside down and shook the kid vigorously and, low and behold, the quarter was coughed up.

"Oh, thank God," the woman said between sobs, "Doctor, I can't thank you enough."

"I'm not a doctor, lady, I work for the Internal Revenue Department."

"It could be just a coincidence, I suppose — but I sometimes wonder if it's the governments way of rubbing it in."

From *Can Board Chairmen Get Measles?* by Charles Preston
Reprinted with permission of Cartoon Features Syndicate of Boston, MA

They say that the only things certain in this world are death and taxes. But it's a shame that they don't come in that order.

✻ ✻ ✻ ✻ ✻

A native Dutchman was describing his flag, the red, white and blue of it: "The colors are just like our taxes," he said, "we turn white when we figure them and blue when we pay them and red when we talk about them."

The American he was talking to said, "That's just like it is in our country. Only when we pay the taxes, we see stars, too."

✻ ✻ ✻ ✻ ✻

Income taxes can be lethal! They are a refutation of the saying that "You can't get killed by a blank."

✻ ✻ ✻ ✻ ✻

A bachelor claimed a son as a tax deduction and the IRS representative asked: "Since you are not married, perhaps your listing of a son is a stenographic error?"

"It most certainly was!" the bachelor replied.

✻ ✻ ✻ ✻ ✻

A citizen sent in his claim for a $95 tax rebate. But he hadn't figured his claim correctly and the IRS returned to him a check for $350. The taxpayer wrote the IRS a letter saying: "Gentlemen: I am now seventy-four years old and finally, at last, I believe in Santa Claus."

✻ ✻ ✻ ✻ ✻

The one thing that makes most of us pay our taxes in due time is that if we don't we will.

✻ ✻ ✻ ✻ ✻

Did you know that April 15 is the same day the *Titanic* went down!

The client was sitting in the office of the IRS man who was examining his Form 1040. The examiner looked up from the papers and said, "Do you want to go over these one-by-one or do you prefer to give up and pay now?"

＊ ＊ ＊ ＊ ＊

Income tax has made more liars out of people than God has.
　　　　　Will Rogers

＊ ＊ ＊ ＊ ＊

There is a special way to determine whether or not you are a success in your business. Ask yourself: "Does it take more money to support the government than my wife?"

＊ ＊ ＊ ＊ ＊

Tax day has been defined as the day the government tells you as follows: "If you haven't spent it by now, you aren't going to spend it."

＊ ＊ ＊ ＊ ＊

Making taxes just and fair is like trying to shoot craps with one die.

＊ ＊ ＊ ＊ ＊

The old man sighed and said, "I quit putting money into the stock market and decided to put it all toward paying income tax, the only thing that's sure to go up."

＊ ＊ ＊ ＊ ＊

A friend asked Jim Peabody why he didn't get a job and stay busy. He replied that today, taxes being what they are, a fellow needs to stay unemployed just to make a living.

＊ ＊ ＊ ＊ ＊

Most men lie on their tax return when they claim to be head of their household!

A fool and his money are soon. . .audited.

＊ ＊ ＊ ＊ ＊

Psychiatry and the IRS have one healing point in common. Both suggest that one shouldn't keep too much to himself.

＊ ＊ ＊ ＊ ＊

One of America's greatest mysteries is the claim that today the dollar is worth only forty cents. Now how could that be when fifty cents out of every dollar goes to pay taxes.

＊ ＊ ＊ ＊ ＊

If the founding fathers of our country thought that taxation without representation was evil, what would they think of it today when we *do* have representation!

" THEY MERGED. NOW THEY TAX YOU TO DEATH."

Some folks think the reason our government is always short of money is because it gets sent in by the U.S. Mail.

＊ ＊ ＊ ＊ ＊

The saying, "My kid is as good as gold" evolved from the deductions allowed on your income tax.

＊ ＊ ＊ ＊ ＊

One result of income taxes is that they transform nest eggs into goose eggs.

＊ ＊ ＊ ＊ ＊

It is a truism that a man owes it to himself to become successful at what he does. But, following that. . .he owes it to the income tax people.

＊ ＊ ＊ ＊ ＊

Most of us still recall the Marx brothers and their wonderful humor. They told this story.

"It's almost April 15th," Groucho said to Chico, "and time to talk about taxes."

"Good. Datsh shust where my friend Ravelli lives," replied Chico.

"You got it wrong, Chico. Not Texas, but taxes. The money we pay the U.S. government."

"Dats eggzactly what I said," argued Chico. "Dallas. .Texas."

＊ ＊ ＊ ＊ ＊

"George? He certainly has done well. Why, he has untold wealth."

"You mean he cheats on his income tax?"

＊ ＊ ＊ ＊ ＊

In levying taxes and in shearing sheep, it is well to stop when you get down to the skin.

Austin O'Malley, 1858-1932

The one thing that hurts more than paying an income tax is not paying an income tax.

Thomas Robert Dewar, 1864-1930

* * * * *

The thing generally raised on city land is taxes.

* * * * *

We owe it to our country to pay our taxes without murmuring. The time to get in our fine work is on the valuation.

Edgar Wilson Nye, 1850-1896

* * * * *

They make attractive cards for all kinds of events, especially for sorrowful ones. So why don't they make a card for April 15th?

* * * * *

Count the day won when, turning on its axis, the earth imposes no additional taxes!

F. P. Adams

* * * * *

Youth today must be strong, unafraid and. . .a better taxpayer than its father.

Henry V. Wade, 1894-?

* * * * *

The art of taxation consists in so plucking the goose as to obtain the largest amount of feathers with the least amount of hissing.

Jean Baptist Colbert, 1619-1683

* * * * *

The income tax could be a lot worse. Suppose we had to pay on what we *think* we're worth?

When it's time for the meek to inherit the earth, their taxes will probably be so high they won't want it.

* * * * *

Death and taxes may be with us always, but death never changes.

* * * * *

Some panhandlers now wear a sign that reads: "It's tax deductible."

* * * * *

A principal fact of keeping a man from holding his own is the Bureau of Internal Revenue.

A California physician claims that prehistoric man was neither stoop-shouldered nor bow-legged. Then came taxes.

* * * * *

The Internal Revenue Department has a fixation, claiming that "Man wants but little here below."

* * * * *

Bureau of Internal Revenue: Institution looking for men who have what it takes in order to take what their fellow men have.

* * * * *

The liquor tax is the only tax that provides its own anesthetic.

* * * * *

Taxpayer: An American who has the government on his payroll.

* * * * *

From Indianapolis: An IRS man was confused by a blank tax return accompanied by this note: "You were notified several times that I have been dead for five years. Please send no more of these blanks."

* * * * *

Herb Shriner thinks Congress will do something about hidden taxes this year. "They won't do away with them," he says, "they'll just hide them better."

* * * * *

Jack Benny once told Jayne Mansfield: "You look like a million bucks, and that's a lot–about $216,000 after taxes."

* * * * *

Ah, for those good old days when Uncle Sam lived within his income–and without most of ours.

Someone once said: "It's better to give than to receive, and it's deductible."

* * * * *

Work hard, save your money, keep on hustling, don't complain, and one day you may be able to pay your taxes in one installment.

* * * * *

It's getting more difficult to support the government in the style to which it has become accustomed.

* * * * *

What do you call a tax evader? An income-poop!

* * * * *

Income tax is the outrageous fine for reckless thriving.

"YOU WON'T FEEL A THING. WE MAKE A SMALL INCISION IN YOUR WALLET AND..."

Suspicion is a major part of some folk's lives. Why, we had a vice-president who wouldn't read any book with a Chapter 11 in it.

* * * * *

I once had a friend who wouldn't watch football games because passes always ended up in the hands of a *receiver*.

* * * * *

One explanation for the U.S. Treasury Form 1040 is that for every $50.00 that you earn, the government keeps $40 and you keep $10.

* * * * *

Undoubtedly, you have heard it before but never with such fervor as said by the Internal Revenue Department: "This is a land of untold wealth!"

* * * * *

It's too bad we cannot invest in taxes. . .they're the one thing sure to go up.

* * * * *

Taxpayer: "I've always paid my taxes once a year."
IRS Rep: "But you can pay them four times a year, four installments, if you wish."
Taxpayer: "I know that. But my heart just can't stand that much strain four times a year!"

* * * * *

There are just two types of Americans who complain about their taxes: Men and women.

* * * * *

A new prayer has been suggested to be used by all adult Americans: "The Lord giveth and the Internal Revenue Service taketh away."

You've simply got to hand it to those collectors employed by the Department of Internal Revenue. Because if you don't, they'll come and get it.

* * * * *

The difference between a Communist government and a democracy like ours is that the Communists won't let you make very much money. But our leaders let you make all the money you can. They just won't let you keep it!

* * * * *

Arthur Godfrey said: "I'm truly proud that I can pay tax money to the government. But I'd be just as proud if the sum were half!"

* * * * *

A successful businessman was about to write a check for his personal income tax. He turned to his secretary and said: "All the results of my success and its rewards. . .I owe to Uncle Sam."

* * * * *

The retired matron's tax return was being reviewed at length by the IRS. Finally, fed up with the lost time and questions, she said, "I certainly wish that you people were as fussy with the people you lend it to."

* * * * *

Two women, employees of the Internal Revenue Service, were sorting through income tax returns. One said to the other: "Hey, Miriam, here's another good one: 'bachelor, no dependents, sixty-five thousand a year!'"

* * * * *

A successful businessman was working at his office desk when his secretary came rushing into the room. "Sir," she exclaimed, "they just came in to see you! An Internal Revenue agent and he's got a gun with him along with a Federal Marshall. They have a subpoena for you, and I don't know how to handle all this. What'll I tell them?"

"Never mind. And thanks a million. But my hiccups quit about five minutes ago. A thousand thanks."

It's been suggested that a theme song be composed for the April 15th "celebration." The title: "Rags to Riches" played in reverse!

* * * * *

It is said that the process of making taxes fair is like a mother trying to give birth to one twin.

* * * * *

It has been remarked that filling out your tax return every year is rather barbaric, much like being kidnapped and then forced to write your own ransom note.

* * * * *

You might as well like violin music because we pay the fiddler whether or not we like it.

Why is it that candidates for the Presidency promise no new taxes but don't say anything about making the old ones higher.

* * * * *

Taxes: The state with lots of oil and some cowboys.

* * * * *

Isn't it amazing how quickly time passes between the due dates of our income tax quarterly payments.

* * * * *

Recently a prominent businessman died. When they probated his will, it read: "Please write a letter to the Internal Revenue Service and include my ashes with it. Send it with my final message: 'Now you have it all.'"

* * * * *

How could our government overlook the one human activity that could bring in ten times present taxes. . .a sin tax.

* * * * *

Taxes are a really odd human responsibility. Why? Because you pay this year's taxes with the money you earned the year before but spent the year before that.

* * * * *

Our government gets a free ride with that class of employees known as taxpayers. Why? Because as government workers, they get no vacation, no sick leave, and no holidays!

* * * * *

Our government should consider the possibility that the American taxpayer may be our first natural resource to be exhausted.

A settler used to be an American pioneer. Now he's the one who paid his taxes!

* * * * *

Sad to say, taxes are merely another form of Capitol punishment.

* * * * *

A bitter taxpayer once said: "We need more watchdogs at the U.S. Treasury and a lot fewer bloodhounds at the Internal Revenue Service."

* * * * *

The value of a dollar today? It is a dime with the balance taken for taxes.

* * * * *

Always remember the ancient adage: When you file your income tax, it is better to give than to deceive.

* * * * *

"Daddy, what's the difference between death and taxes that you talk about so much?"
"Well, son, let me put it this way: Death doesn't get worse every time the U.S. Congress meets."

* * * * *

"Don't you find filling out the income tax form a difficult thing?"
"I sure do. It's that way with all my friends, too."
"There's only one person who has no trouble filling out her form."
"Really? Who's that?"
"Dolly Parton!"

"When did you first notice you didn't enjoy making people squirm?"

"How's your husband?"

"He's a wild man. Absolutely wild today. He just mailed in his income tax."

❋ ❋ ❋ ❋ ❋

"Untold wealth" is that which does not appear on the income tax.

5
BANKS and BANKING

A prosperous-looking fellow parked his Rolls Royce, then walked into the bank and on into the president's office. "I'd like to borrow six thousand dollars for a month," he told the President.

"Very good," replied the president. "Have you collateral for the loan?"

"Yes. My Rolls Royce is parked outside in your lot. Here are the keys."

The fellow got his money and left, only to return a month later to pay off the loan. He did just that and was about to leave the bank when the president of the bank asked: "Since you are obviously well off, why did you borrow this trivial sum for such a short time?"

"Where else could I park my Rolls Royce for a month for only $40?"

✳ ✳ ✳ ✳ ✳

In some cases, it's better to give than to lend because it costs almost the same.

✳ ✳ ✳ ✳ ✳

The guy was very frugal, kept almost all of his paycheck deposited in his hometown bank. He rarely wrote a check on his account but one time he decided to go to Chicago and live it up. And he did. He paid his hotel room and meals there with a check but it bounced, being returned: "Not Sufficient Funds." He called the bank and asked, "How come? I've been sending money to my checking account in your bank for years. And I rarely write a check. How come I'm NSF?"

The teller replied, "The fact that your check was returned for 'Not Sufficient Funds' doesn't mean that you don't have the money. It means *we* don't!"

Bank talk is really a gas! Why, when you go to a bank, you hear talk of redemption and more talk about conversion... why, a person would think he was in church!

* * * * *

One thing is sure. . .a fool and his money are soon audited.

* * * * *

It's been said that "America is the only place in the world where you can borrow $20,000 from a relative, get a $75,000 first mortgage, then a second mortgage for $40,000 and claim to be called a homeowner!

* * * * *

Johnny Carson once remarked: "You can get more with a kind word and a gun than you can with a kind word alone."

* * * * *

After they bought the new home with the 15-year mortgage, the husband told his wife that it needed lots of repairs but that he planned to do all of them himself on weekends. "And I tell you this. . .if I work every weekend for the life of that loan, I just might be able to get our house in shape to sell it."

* * * * *

Someone described a bank as a pawnshop with suits and manicures.

* * * * *

On a loan officer's desk, there is a sign reading, "In this office, in this bank, 'no' is a hundred percent complete sentence."

* * * * *

The best way to bury an account is with little digs.

"YOU INVESTED IN A COIN LAUNDRY AT A NUDIST COLONY?"

"I HOPE YOU DON'T MIND BUT IT SEEMS TO BRING BETTER RESULTS THAN FRIENDLY REMINDERS."

The bank's president was talking to one of the junior officers when the latter's phone rang. The junior officer kept saying, "No. . .no. . .yes. . .no. . .no!" and then hung up. The president asked: "John, what did you say 'yes' to?"

"Not to worry, Sir," said the other. "It was only when he asked if I was still listening that I said, 'yes'."

* * * * *

Mark Twain said it all when he judged a banker in this way: "A banker is a fellow who lends you his umbrella when the sun is shining and wants it back the minute it begins to rain!"

* * * * *

Debt is the sure and certain outcome of an uncertain income.

* * * * *

Things were really tough at this particular bank. So the president went to a hardware store and bought one hundred garden rakes. A few days later, he was back to buy another fifty at the same price. . .$10.00 each. The salesman at the store asked what he was doing with so many rakes and the banker said, "We sell them for $5.00."

"For $5.00?" the salesman said, aghast. "How can you pay $10.00 and then sell them for $5.00. You lose money on every sale."

"It beats banking," was the reply.

* * * * *

When and where money talks, almost nobody pays attention to the grammar.

* * * * *

The credit manager for a tent manufacturing company had borrowed $500,000 from the bank with the understanding that the debt would be paid off in six months. Due date was tomorrow and the guy could not sleep the night before. He paced the floor in his bedroom.

"Come to bed, Honey," his wife said.

"I can't sleep. I'm too worried about the debt we owe. It's due tomorrow."

"Why didn't you pay off the debt?"

"Because we didn't have the money."

"Then don't pay it back."

"But I've got to! It's the bank's money."

"In that case, come to bed and let them walk the floor."

✳ ✳ ✳ ✳ ✳

Someone defined civilization as a human condition where nothing can get done without first securing financing.

✳ ✳ ✳ ✳ ✳

A frequent dealer with banks once remarked that she preferred automated tellers to the genuine bank tellers because they had more personality!

✳ ✳ ✳ ✳ ✳

"I'm convinced that a banker is only a pawnbroker in a three-piece suit," said the businessman after completing his loan.

✳ ✳ ✳ ✳ ✳

Is it possible that the reason banks have drive-up tellers is so that the cars can see their real owners?

✳ ✳ ✳ ✳ ✳

It has been said that a bank is a lending institution where you can borrow money, providing you give them sufficient evidence that you don't really need it.

✳ ✳ ✳ ✳ ✳

Elmer Jorgensen, well into his seventies, had refused to retire. Finally, he came to the president of his company and said, "Boss, I'm ready to retire now. Is that OK with you?"

The boss replied, "You know it is, Elmer. I've been after you to retire for several years now. What made you suddenly agree to do it?"

"Well, last week, I looked out on my front lawn and there was a flock of vultures out there. Every day their number increased, so. . .I figure, well, you know how it is!"

"Is that the only reason?" the boss asked.

"Well, no," the old man replied. "For one thing, my kids have all begun to look middle-aged. . .most of the names in my customer book now end with MD and now we've got too damned much room in our house and not enough in the medicine cabinet. Understand?"

His boss nodded and grinned.

✳ ✳ ✳ ✳ ✳

A few businesses are out just for the money. Their only interest in the customer is as the courier from the former to the bank.

"WHAT EXACTLY IS 'ONE AND A HALF SMACKEROOS'?"

"NO SIR, I DON'T BELIEVE I CARE TO GO DOUBLE OR NOTHING."

The chief bookkeeper is brought into the president's office where he's told, "Sam, there is $75,000 missing from our main safe and you and I alone know the combination. What have you got to say?"

"Just this, Sir. Let's you and me each chip in $37,500 and just forget the entire matter!"

❋ ❋ ❋ ❋ ❋

Isn't it a shame that the loan officer in our bank is not the advertising man?

❋ ❋ ❋ ❋ ❋

The bank president was annoyed at the sudden noises that had erupted outside his office. He folded the work on his desk and strode outside to the lobby where he saw the first vice-president.

"What's all this noise about out here," he exclaimed. "I

can't work, there's so much bedlam!"

"There's a bank robbery in process," said the V.P.

"What a relief!" exclaimed the president. "I thought it was a hostile takeover!"

* * * * *

Question: How many *bankers*. . .does it take to screw in a lightbulb?

Answer: Four. One to hold the bulb and three to try to remember the combination.

* * * * *

"I worked for twenty years, always moving up in my bank. Then I became cashier. Then I moved on."

"Really? And what did you move on to?"

"Jail."

* * * * *

The best way to get a dead-beat to pay you is to notify all the other creditors that he did!

* * * * *

A department store owner called his bank and asked for an extension on a five-hundred-thousand-dollar loan.

"No! Sorry, but no!" the bank president said. "Pay today or else!"

"Have you ever been in the department store business?" the owner asked.

"No! Never!"

"Well, tomorrow you will be," replied the borrower.

* * * * *

The credit of an individual is the only commodity that gets better the less it's used.

The elderly woman and customer of the First State Bank was furious at receiving an overdraft statement. She called the president of the bank and asked, "How much did I have in the bank at the end of last month?"

"You had a five-hundred-dollar balance," the president said.

"And did I send you a letter about it?" she exclaimed.

＊ ＊ ＊ ＊ ＊

Pete Smith finally got a bank to loan him enough money to keep his business going. After he signed the papers, he turned to leave, smiling broadly. "I can't thank you and the bank enough," he said. "I'll be eternally indebted to you." And he means it.

＊ ＊ ＊ ＊ ＊

Someone has defined a bank as a place that keeps your money until tax time.

＊ ＊ ＊ ＊ ＊

The lad applied to a bank for a job, his first try since graduating from college. "What kind of job did you have in mind?" the employment officer at the bank asked.

"How about starting as vice-president?" the young man said.

"Ridiculous! We have twelve of them already," was the response.

"Don't let that worry you," the lad responded. "I'm not superstitious."

＊ ＊ ＊ ＊ ＊

How can I trust a bank to keep my money safe when it has dozens of pens stolen every day?

＊ ＊ ＊ ＊ ＊

Sometimes profanity has its place. Consider this situation:

A man staggered into the bank and up to a cashier's window. "I got some money and want to open a goddam checking account."

The cashier glanced at the man saying, "I beg your

pardon?"

"I said open up your goddam window and open a goddam account for me."

The clerk shook his head. "Sir, this is a fine, reputable bank. We don't allow that kind of language to be used here." He slammed shut the window with a bang!

The bank president heard the commotion and came running up to the cashier's window. "What's going on here?" the president said. "What's all the ruckus about?"

The customer said, "I just won a goddam five million dollars in the sonofabitchin' lottery and I want to open a damn bank account."

The bank president smiled, saying, "And is our employee, the sonofabitch, givin' you a hard time?"

✳ ✳ ✳ ✳ ✳

Money isn't everything. . .as long as you have enough.
Malcolm Forbes

Two friends walked out of church one Sunday morning and they were discussing the biblical theme of the sermon: Noah. "My Dad told me that Noah was the greatest financier that ever lived," one fellow said.

"I never heard about that," the other man replied. "Just how did he manage to be a financier?" the other man asked.

"Simple. He floated a brand new company when the entire world was in liquidation!"

✳ ✳ ✳ ✳ ✳

From the Clifton Forge, VA *Daily Review*:
Save regularly in our bank. You'll never reget it.

✳ ✳ ✳ ✳ ✳

Experience may be the best teacher, but it's often late to school.

"*I TELL PEOPLE THAT I'M IN THE BANKING BUSINESS.*"

The bank's new employee was so fast at counting money, at moving money in and out of the drawer and at everything that he did that the bank president was invited over to watch him. And the president was truly impressed. He asked the fellow: "You're the fastest man we've ever had as a bank teller, Sir. Where did you learn to move so fast?"

"Yale."

"Interesting. And what's your name?"

"Yackson."

* * * * *

The safest way to make money is to fold it over once and put in your pocket.
　　　　　Kim Hubbard

* * * * *

Isn't it amazing that the banks chain down their pens but loan billions to Third World countries?

* * * * *

Somebody once described a banker as a pawnbroker wearing a three-piece suit and button-down collar. . .with tie!

* * * * *

Did you hear about the South American manufacturer who asked for six American bankers to serve as pallbearers? He said it was only fair that, since they'd carried him this long, they should be allowed to finish the job.

* * * * *

An old friend of mine lately appeared more and more preoccupied, and so I asked him about his problem.

"It's my bank. Where I work. We're in more and more trouble. Now we're going through a complete reorganization."

"What went wrong?"

"It seems that we've got more vice-presidents than depositors."

"I know how proud of it you are Hodgekiss, but—"

From *Can Board Chairmen Get Measles?* by Charles Preston
Reprinted with permission of Cartoon Features Syndicate of Boston, MA

"WHO'S HUMMING 'SOUTH OF THE BORDER?'"

The old saying has it: "Better to give than to lend."
They should have added, "And it costs about the same."

＊ ＊ ＊ ＊ ＊

Let us all be happy and live within our means. . .even if we
have to borrow money to do it.
Artemus Ward

"HOW SMALL DO I HAVE TO BE TO GET SOME MONEY"

Emil Jurgens needed money in his business so he went to
his banker, an elderly gent with a hearing aid. "I need to
borrow three thousand dollars," Emil said.
"How much do you need? Please repeat that. I'm a bit
hard of hearing."

"I need four thousand dollars."
"I still can't hear you. Say it again in my other ear."
"I said I need seven thousand dollars at once."
Once more: "Louder."
Emil shouted: "I need ten thousand dollars, Sir!"
"Mister," the banker said, "Let's go back to my three thousand dollar ear."

❊ ❊ ❊ ❊ ❊

If a banker writes a bad poem, nobody says anything. But if a poor poet writes a bad check, all hell breaks loose.

❊ ❊ ❊ ❊ ❊

THE MAN AT THE DESK

I

The Man at the Desk has a patient look
As he writes and writes in his copybook,
And he bends his back to the task before
Like a galley slave to his hand-rubbed oar.
Columns of figures he marshals by,
Piled up decimals mountains high,
Which seem to sing to his well-ruled brain
His long, monotonous life-refrain:-

"Debit, credit, voucher, pay,-
Discount, balance, day by day,
Carried forward, interest, duns,"-
So the monotonous river runs.

II

The Man at the Desk with the patient look
Has followed the rule of the copybook:
"Early to bed and early to rise,"
Yet he's neither healthy, wealthy, nor wise.
Honest, industrious, sober, chained
To his office cell he has long remained,
Dear of ambition, busy of pen,
Adding up figues for other men.

"Debit, credit, remit, amount,
Carried forward, close account;
Daybooks, draftbook, interest, duns,"-
So the monotonous river runs.

III

The Man at the Desk with the patient look
Has written his life in the open book.
Has charged up Youth with a small amount,
And crossed off Love as a closed account;
Yet bright are the tears in his faded eye
As the column of figures marches by,
Black of ink and with mourning brave,
Like a last parade to a yawning grave.

"Debit, credit," the bugles play,
"Discount, balance, voucher, pay,
Carried forward, interest, duns,"–
So the monotonous river runs.

Random Rhymes and Odd Numbers
by Wallace Irwin.
Norwood Press, Norwood, MA: 1906

Problem Solving Flow Chart

From *Nothing Serious - Just A Little Chat With The Boss*
Reprinted by permission of Ann E Weeks, DNS
Passage Publishing, Inc. - Louisville, KY

6

WORKERS, LABORERS, and OTHER "GET-IT-DONER'S"

The Standard Bicycle Manufacturing Company was giving a retirement banquet to the man who had been treasurer of the company for forty years. At the conclusion of the dinner, he was asked to say a few words. "Ladies and Gentlemen," he began. "I was asked by the president of our great company to discuss my success as treasurer of this company, how I did it and the principles behind my doing it, and things like that. Well, I thought I'd stick with how I managed to be a successful treasurer. . .the secret of my success. It all started last summer when I attended a carnival in my small hometown. I was watching a strong man--part of a circus performance-- squeeze a lemon to the last drop. When he'd finished, he invited anyone to come up and try to get more out of that lemon. I stepped forward, took the lemon, and squeezed at least a tablespoonful more out of it. The strong man was astounded. He said, 'In twenty years of doing that squeeze job, I never had a soul try it after me who could get a single drop. You got a tablespoonful. How did you do it?'

I said. . .'Well, I must tell you that I've been treasurer of the Standard Bicycle Company for forty years! That explains my success!'"

❋ ❋ ❋ ❋ ❋

Charlie Stevens was the tallest, broadest man in the entire company. They said his feet were so big he had to pull his pants on over his head.

❋ ❋ ❋ ❋ ❋

"Why does the company coffee taste so bad?" one employee asked while in the company cafeteria.

"I think it's because it's a blend," his friend said.

"That shouldn't make any difference. I always use a blend at home."

"Yeah, I know," his friend replied. "But this is not the same. This is a blend of yesterday's and today's."

What does it all signify when a person reports to a boss who gives them encouragement, support, understanding, and respect? Usually it means that, somehow or other, they've gotten into the wrong office.

❊ ❊ ❊ ❊ ❊

Talk about an unreasonable boss! Listen to this! Mary Alphonse asked her boss for a day off so that she could observe and celebrate her silver wedding anniversary. And do you know what her boss told her? "Tell me, Mrs. Alphonse. . .are you going to burden me with this every twenty-five years?"

❊ ❊ ❊ ❊ ❊

We learn from experience that men never learn anything from experience.
George Bernard Shaw

❊ ❊ ❊ ❊ ❊

You ask if I'm upset about these tough economic times. I'm not. Heck, man, I didn't have any more money when times were good!

❊ ❊ ❊ ❊ ❊

Peter was hard at his new job with a large corporation but found the pretty women who worked there a most disconcerting distraction. He went to his supervisor and told him the trouble he was having getting accustomed to working, surrounded by lovely ladies.

"Peter," the supervisor said, "stand fast. Pay them no attention. Keep your mind on your business and you'll be rewarded in heaven."

Peter stayed on the job but the situation got no better and he was about to break down and start making passes at some of the girls.

At about that time, his superior happened by and Peter told him that he just couldn't take the "hands off" attitude any longer.

"But you must," his supervisor warned. "You'll get your reward in heaven, just as I told you before."

"And just what," asked Peter, "will that reward be?"

"A bucket of oats, jackass!" a nearby worker yelled over.

The salary we dreamed of fifteen years ago, we can't live on today.

✳ ✳ ✳ ✳ ✳

Success is the ability to keep your obituary up-to-date!

✳ ✳ ✳ ✳ ✳

Success is sweet but its secret is sweat.

✳ ✳ ✳ ✳ ✳

The young man stood before the personnel manager and looked extremely puzzled after the personnel manager asked him: "Young man, what have you done?"
He scratched his head and then replied, "Sir, about what?"

✳ ✳ ✳ ✳ ✳

Problems are only opportunities with thorns on them.

NEWS WARNS OF SHORTAGE OF CLEAN AIR
AND CERTAIN SPECIES IN DECLINE.
BUT(T) THERE'S NO SHORTAGE ANYWHERE
OF OFFICIALS COVERING THEIR BE-HINDS.

© 1995, J. R. DUNN, JRDISM-66, HUMOR & HEALTH JJOURNAL
JACKSON, MS 37236-6814

181

Gambling is the only business that I know of where dissatisfied customers keep coming back.
Bill Cosby

＊ ＊ ＊ ＊ ＊

Monday is an awful way to spend one seventh of your entire life.

＊ ＊ ＊ ＊ ＊

A sexy outfit is not proper for a women in the workplace. Unfortunately, some women seem to have been poured into their dress but forgot to say "when."

＊ ＊ ＊ ＊ ＊

A view of our moral standards is offered in the fact that workers who take office supplies home for personal use are not considered criminals. They consider their theft as merely a "fringe benefit."

＊ ＊ ＊ ＊ ＊

A pension is when you get paid for a service you don't do any more. It's a little like alimony!

＊ ＊ ＊ ＊ ＊

Suggestion boxes are fine. . .a good and venerable idea. But ours never seems to be looked at by the bosses. The last time they opened our suggestion box, they took out a yellowed paper that had on it the suggestion that employees drive two-wheeled buggies instead of four wheelers to save space in the parking lot.

＊ ＊ ＊ ＊ ＊

A disappointed employee said to his boss: "Sir, I feel terrible about not getting that job. I dreamed about getting it night and day!"
"I know. That was the trouble. You were supposed to be working."

There's an office maxim where I work. It says: "Don't believe everything you hear. Get it out of your mind! Just pass it on to somebody else!"

✳ ✳ ✳ ✳ ✳

The retiree stood to make his "thank you" speech following the dinner given in his honor. "There's just one thing I want to say to all you nice people whom I've known for so many years. I appreciate the pension you've given me. It's enough to last me for the rest of my life. . .unless I want to buy something."

✳ ✳ ✳ ✳ ✳

When it comes to giving to charity at our office, we have this one jerk who stops at nothing!

✳ ✳ ✳ ✳ ✳

My boss is intolerable. But that's his only fault.

✳ ✳ ✳ ✳ ✳

There's no doubt in the company's responsibility to contribute to your income when you are old and feeble. Heck fire, they made you that way.

✳ ✳ ✳ ✳ ✳

Some employees answer the telephone as if they've just had their request for a day off turned down.

✳ ✳ ✳ ✳ ✳

Don't let yourself get frantic just because you have a boss who runs things with a barbed iron fist. Just relax and hope that he'll get jock itch!

✳ ✳ ✳ ✳ ✳

Someone said that a congressman has suggested changing the national motto from "E Pluribus Unum" to "Put it on my tab."

IMPRESS-THE-BOSS KIT

Bob: Friends, does it seem like you're always being passed over at the office when the time comes for a promotion?

Ray: Do you just go on doing the same job year after year, always efficient, but never conspicuous?

Bob: Well, neighbors, it doesn't have to be that way. Quick success can be yours now, with the wonderful Bob and Ray Impress-the-Boss Kit.

Ray: Here in one neat package is everything you need to convince your employers that you are the most diligent and valuable worker in the organization.

Bob: For example, the kit contains a generous three-ounce bottle of Bob and Ray eyedrops. These drops are guaranteed to make your eyes bloodshot, and lend credence to the story that you've been taking work home from the office and doing without sleep.

Ray: There's also a handy length of rubber tubing which can be run from your desk to the water cooler. Naturally, the boss will inquire about this. . .and a promotion is virtually insured when you inform him that you don't have time to leave your desk to get a drink of water!

Bob: Here, too, in this Impress-the-Boss Kit, is an ample jar of white make-up, guaranteed to give you a beautiful office pallor. After all, nobody's going to promote a healthy-looking specimen who appears to spend half his waking hours on the golf course.

Ray: And looking through the lower shelf of the kit, here I see that we have an atomizer filled with glycerine, which can be used to spray beads of sweat on your forehead. Every boss likes to see his employees sweating on the job.

Bob: A worried expression of concern can also go a long way toward winning you that much-wanted promotion-- and the indelible make-up pencil included with each kit will enable you to have deeply etched furrows in your brow at all times.

Ray: Naturally, you'll want your employer to think that you don't have time to go out for lunch, and so each Bob and Ray Impress-the-Boss Kit contains an artificial plastic sandwich in your choice of either ham or cheese. You'll be proud to display this handsome lifelike sandwich on your desk at all times.

Bob: Yes, friends, there's just about everything in this kit to

Ray: We could read endless letters here from our files telling how our kit enabled shipping clerks to become steel company presidents, and garbage men to become sanitation officials. But I'm sure the value of the kit is obvious to you without these testimonials.

Bob: Certainly you'll want an Impress-the-Boss Kit for your very own, so why not act quickly and take advantage of our special bonus offer?

Ray: If your order is postmarked before midnight tonight, you'll receive, at no additional charge, three simulated job-offer letters.

Bob: These letters, which can be left around where the boss will see them, supposedly offer you jobs from other companies for much more money than you are now making.

Ray: When the boss sees these letters, he'll realize that he must promote you quickly, in order to keep a valuable worker.

Bob: Or he may fire you for disloyalty to his firm, but in any event you'll want to get more information about this offer before midnight tonight.

Ray: Just address your inquiry to: "Gold Brick," in care of Bob and Ray, New York.

❋ ❋ ❋ ❋ ❋

We've started a club for employees in our company who spend too much time talking on the phone. We named the club "ON-AND-ON-ANONYMOUS!"

❋ ❋ ❋ ❋ ❋

You can be sure that when an executive tells you, "You'll get this when hell freezes over" that he really means three days *after* hell freezes over.

In a report to higher authority, the difference between "date of completion" and "scheduled date of completion" is something like the difference between "chicken" and "chicken pox!"

✻ ✻ ✻ ✻ ✻

Most reports to higher authority in the company consist of three parts: what you know, what you think you know, and what the boss wants to hear.

✻ ✻ ✻ ✻ ✻

The boss called an assistant to his office and told her, "Here's the outline of your report. You have three days to finish it."

The assistant said, "Good. I'll take Thanksgiving, New Year's and Christmas!"

"WE'D LIKE TO PAY YOU WHAT YOU'RE WORTH, TOO, FENSTROM. UNFORTUNATELY, WE MUST CONFORM TO THE MINIMUM WAGE LAW."

It seems a truism that today's office furniture was designed *by* asses but certainly not *for* them.

* * * * *

The personnel office of a large factory was checking on a particular job application. They called the place of previous employment and asked: "Was he steady on the job?"

"Steady?" came the reply. "You bet he was. Why that man was practically motionless!"

* * * * *

Our office is composed of a truly inefficient bunch of people. It took them three weeks to discover that the "OUT" basket was missing.

* * * * *

The last time I called in sick, my boss demanded that I bring a note from my doctor. Wasn't a problem at all because my doctor plays in my foursome!

* * * * *

There are some promotions that come with a pay raise and some that don't. "With" is better.

* * * * *

I want to announce that as of the first of the month, the entire operation of our company will go on automation.

Murmurings were heard throughout the assembled workers until the president raised his hand to silence them. "Not a single worker will be laid off and wages will not change. Bonuses will be just as before along with holidays with pay, sick benefits, and pension plans. Everyone of you will be expected to appear at the usual hour for work on Wednesday of each week. Wednesday only."

There was a total hush. Then a voice intruded on the silence: "You mean. . .you mean. . .every doggone Wednesday?"

Reports to higher executives are like bikinis. What they reveal is interesting but what they conceal is vital.

❋ ❋ ❋ ❋ ❋

This particular office worker had been falsifying his tax return for years, until the revenue office finally caught up with him. An agent came to his house and said, "Yes, Mr. Jones, we *do* want to make a federal case of it!"

❋ ❋ ❋ ❋ ❋

There is a sign on the wall of a famous New York newspaper stating: "There is no such thing as petty cash!" Beneath it is written: "THERE IS NO SUCH THING AS CASH!"

❋ ❋ ❋ ❋ ❋

An assistant to the boss was sent out to ask employees about certain wage proposals the boss was going to offer them. The assistant returned with the results and explained them to the boss as follows: "It's OK with them to have a guaranteed annual wage and a guaranteed annual bonus along with the guaranteed pension plan," the emissary told the boss, "only they all said they'd like to have a guarantee that you won't go broke!"

❋ ❋ ❋ ❋ ❋

Inflation isn't all bad, you know. For example, inflation allows employees to live in better, more exclusive neighborhoods without ever moving.

❋ ❋ ❋ ❋ ❋

Extreme wealth used to be a status symbol. Now you need it just to make ends meet.

❋ ❋ ❋ ❋ ❋

At our regular Monday morning meeting, the boss passed a sign around. It read: "THE EASIEST WAY TO MAKE ENDS MEET IS TO GET OFF YOUR OWN!"

188

The worst aspect of being low man on the totem pole is that you have so many wooden-headed bastards frowning down on you. And if you look up, all that you see are asses!

※ ※ ※ ※ ※

An office worker was having a hard time making ends meet on his salary. He asked an accountant how he could, in the future, estimate the cost of living. He was told: "Take your income, whatever it may be, and add twenty-five percent."

※ ※ ※ ※ ※

Harry Truman stated it most trenchantly: "When your neighbor loses his job, it's a recession. But when you lose yours. . .it's a depression!"

Retirement signifies that you are free to do nothing all day and, what's more, you don't have to show up at the office to do it!

✳ ✳ ✳ ✳ ✳

Left wingers say that there are two classes of workers in America: Those who make their living from the sweat of their brows and those who then sell them cold drinks, paper towels, and air conditioners.

✳ ✳ ✳ ✳ ✳

At his retirement party, the boss gave the retiree the large wall clock that hung in the employee's office and then said: "George, you've watched the clock so much all the years you worked here that we think you should take it home with you!"

✳ ✳ ✳ ✳ ✳

How long have I worked for this company? Well, let me put it this way. . .when I started here the Dead Sea was only sick!

✳ ✳ ✳ ✳ ✳

This guy is the kind of fellow who can do nothing right. Every office has one, the kind of guy who climbs the ladder of success wrong by wrong!

✳ ✳ ✳ ✳ ✳

Talk about addiction to something. We have this guy in our office who is so addicted to tea that his blood type is listed as Lipton's.

✳ ✳ ✳ ✳ ✳

An executive was lecturing a group of junior executives on how to get ahead in the company. "Don't drink, don't smoke, eat only simple foods. Get plenty of exercise and sleep. Thus, even if you don't live a long life, it'll certainly seem that you did!"

At lunch, a group of employees were discussing the ravages of inflation on their paychecks. One man confided: "We've found a way to get ahead of it," he said, "at the first of the month when I get my paycheck, I give it to my wife. She spends it during the first week, before it loses its purchasing power!"

* * * * *

My company is just great. . .and so considerate. They started an aerobics class for employees and I love it. My pulse starts pounding, and my heart races and races, and I break into a heavy sweat. . .and that's just from watching the women!

* * * * *

Isn't it interesting how an executive knows a bit about everything while his assistant knows everything about a bit but the receptionist knows all about everything.

* * * * *

The only way to keep your health is to eat what you don't want, drink what you don't like, and do what you'd rather not.
Mark Twain

* * * * *

Experience is that superb knowledge that lets you know when you've repeated that same damned mistake.

* * * * *

Today, the work ethic is very different from that of a generation ago. Why I recall my father telling me that he once turned down a job working six days a week, ten hours a day, because he wasn't looking for a part-time job!

* * * * *

Don't be looking around for better opportunities all the time. Think of it this way: "A grapefruit is a lemon that took advantage of its opportunities!"

So be a smart grapefruit and stay where you are and keep your eyes open!

✳ ✳ ✳ ✳ ✳

They hired a new brain in our office. And I tell you that jerk is all brains! He even has to be careful just how he sits down.

✳ ✳ ✳ ✳ ✳

Some people are perennially late. We had this one girl in the office who was that type. But the boss was lenient with her. When she'd been with the company twenty-five years, they waited another ten and celebrated the twenty-fifth anniversary on the thirty-fifth year just to be consistent.

✳ ✳ ✳ ✳ ✳

Thank God for golf. It makes going back to work on Monday a genuine relief!

✳ ✳ ✳ ✳ ✳

When the Red Cross comes to our office to solicit blood, this one guy, a very heavy drinker, doesn't donate the customary pint of blood. He donates a FIFTH!

✳ ✳ ✳ ✳ ✳

Just remember that average is merely the best of the lousy and the lousiest of the best.

✳ ✳ ✳ ✳ ✳

This jerk who works with me has a sure system for saving money. He forgets from whom he borrows it!

✳ ✳ ✳ ✳ ✳

Many offices have trouble-makers. This one guy in our office said he thought of us all as brothers. "Yeah," sneered one fellow who knew him well, "Brothers! Maybe Cain and Abel?"

The one thing that's wrong with a pension is that you've got no one to go to for a raise.

* * * * *

The guy that works next to me drinks too darned much. And his wife has had about enough of it, threatening divorce. So the other night this guy came in about three in the morning, saying, "Honey, I hope you didn't pay my kidnappers any ransom money!" But it didn't work.

* * * * *

This guy, the office cheapskate, squeezes a nickel so hard that he castrated the buffalo!

* * * * *

My boss is entirely bald. . .not a strand of hair above his ears. He always says that God made every head in this world. Those he was ashamed of, he covered with a full--and then some--head of hair.

* * * * *

This new employee we've got is really dumb. Why the first day on the job, we had to show him how the wastebasket worked!

* * * * *

The personnel office of the large manufacturing company got a call from another company's personnel office inquiring about a former employee. "How long did Elmer Jones work for you, Sir?" the voice asked.
"Oh, three days," was the reply.
"But the applicant states that he worked three years for you."
"That's just it. That's all he ever worked!"

* * * * *

My boss has a slick way of determining whom he really needs. He gives us all long vacations!

J.L. PALTROW
—
PRESIDENT

" ROBERTS, WHAT'S THIS I HEAR ABOUT
YOU WINNING SOME LOTTERY ? "

My boss likes to appear as a real tough, physically powerful guy. But we all know he really was a bouncer once. . .in a salad bar.

* * * * *

Sally Restudnik retired after forty years of working for the same company. When asked how she liked all her new free time, she replied, "It's OK but I sure hate drinking coffee on my own time."

* * * * *

The new fellow in our office is the dumbest thing we've seen. He's so dumb that if you gave him three guesses, he couldn't tell you which way the elevator was going.

* * * * *

Mary Ellen, the boss's secretary, is so thin that when she swallowed an olive, three of the company's men left town.

Susie Plumber claims she's a virgin and I believe her. You know why? Because she told me that she was going to take music lessons in order to learn how to fiddle around.

✳ ✳ ✳ ✳ ✳

Is my boss considerate? You bet he is! Why, he lets me come in any time I want before nine and leave any time I'm of a mind to after five.

✳ ✳ ✳ ✳ ✳

Two men who worked in the accounting department were at the drinking fountain, talking, when a new office employee walked by swinging her hips gracefully. "Hey, man," the one fellow said, "that new girl may not know a debit from a credit but she sure as heck adds up!"

✳ ✳ ✳ ✳ ✳

This guy that works with me, Florin Barker, is one dumb jerk. He thinks a Band-Aid is a charitable organization for musicians.

✳ ✳ ✳ ✳ ✳

Nobody has ever drowned in sweat.

✳ ✳ ✳ ✳ ✳

Retirement doesn't please all wives. No, Sir! Some say, "I married him for better or worse but I did not marry him expecting him for lunch every. . .damn. . .day!"

✳ ✳ ✳ ✳ ✳

You ask how I did in the stock market this year? Let me explain it this way, I've switched brokers . . .from stock to pawn.

✳ ✳ ✳ ✳ ✳

This guy who works two desks away recently had a boat accident that proves his conceit. He was hit by a boat while taking a walk on water (he said).

The guy didn't want to retire, saying: "Heck, boss, I can do the very same things today that I did when I was eighteen!"

His boss replied: "Then you must have been one heluva jerk at eighteen!"

* * * * *

Many say they can do the same things at 65 that they did at thirty. Only now, they take a nap after each do!

* * * * *

The guy who works at the desk next to mine is a true cheapskate. He refused to buy an Easter Seal until I convinced him that he wouldn't have to feed it.

* * * * *

It's true that computers don't have what we call intelligence. But they do have a sensible substitute for it, best illustrated in the fact that they don't make an ass out of themselves at the office Christmas party.

"YOU CAN ALWAYS TELL THE MARRIED GUYS. THEY'RE THE ONES WHO WORK LATE."

A truck driver pulled in at a roadside diner, walked into the place, and ordered a hamburger, cup of coffee, and piece of pie. He had just begun to eat when four tough-looking men in painted leather jackets parked outside then walked inside the eatery. One grabbed the truck driver's hamburger and began to eat it, another drank his coffee, and another grabbed his pie. Wisely, the truck driver said not a word, got up, walked to the cashier, paid, and left. One of the motorcyclists said, "He's a real pantywaist, ain't he." The cashier heard him and said, "He's a lousy driver, too. He just ran over four motorcycles parked outside."

✳ ✳ ✳ ✳ ✳

Wouldn't it be grand if we could sell our experience for what it cost us!

✳ ✳ ✳ ✳ ✳

A government report is just out that states that the federal government takes about 50% of the working man's salary. That seems an incredible tax, doesn't it? Stop to consider that God Himself expects only 10%.

You know that inflation has overtaken the economy when you figure that even muggers will not accept cash!

* * * * *

If a raise is a reward for past performance, how come it is never retroactive?

* * * * *

"I always show up at the office religiously," the guy told me, "once a week!"

* * * * *

Pete Akers handles all our postage. Pete is one of those guys who is terribly fat, or, if you prefer, overweight. We could never get him to try a diet until he found out that his bathtub was formfitting. That did it.

* * * * *

If you are the kind of person who keeps his nose to the grindstone, his shoulder to the wheel, and his best foot forward, you have got to have a coffee break. Why? Because you'll never be able to swallow in that position.

* * * * *

I have a really trivial job at the office. As a result I have a parking space so far from my office that I pass my house on the way from the space to my office.

* * * * *

The boys were discussing what they had for breakfast. One guy said, "I never talk about my wife's coffee. Y'know why? Well, I might be old and weak myself someday."

* * * * *

This one guy who works with me spent most of his savings sending his boy through college. "Was it worth it?" I asked him. "You bet it was," he replied. "That kid of mine can now write stuff on toilet walls in three languages."

The EATRITE restaurant was having trouble hiring experienced waiters and finally settled for a guy whose sole experience was as a salesman in a pawnshop. The first night on the job, the new waiter proved himself. The customer pleaded inability to pay for his meal, after eating it. The waiter said, "That's not so bad. We'll just write your name on the wall and you can pay the next time you come to eat here."

"But everybody'll see it," said the customer.

"Not to worry," the waiter assured him. "Nobody'll see it because your overcoat'll be hanging over it."

✳ ✳ ✳ ✳ ✳

Things are so bad in this country that they've even reduced the wages of sin.

✳ ✳ ✳ ✳ ✳

The barroom waitress asked--no demanded--a vacation. "I need it, now!" she demanded.

Her boss asked: "Why now?"

"Because I don't look so good now. I ain't myself."

"You look great to me. Why do you say that?"

"Because the businessmen are starting to count their change."

✳ ✳ ✳ ✳ ✳

Experience is generally what you get when you're expecting something better.

✳ ✳ ✳ ✳ ✳

God created the world in six days, the Bible tells us. And a good thing there were no unions then. Otherwise, when God said, "Let there be light!" the shop steward would have said, "Hey now. . .YOU just wait a goldarned minute!"

✳ ✳ ✳ ✳ ✳

Science tells us that the amoeba is the lowest form of life. Probably that's because they never considered shop stewards.

"Wilkins never wastes a minute, J.P. —that's his lunch."

From *Can Board Chairmen Get Measles?* by Charles Preston
Reprinted with permission of Cartoon Features Syndicate of Boston, MA

Good workers never put off until tomorrow doing a job that needs doing. . .if they can get someone else to do it!

＊ ＊ ＊ ＊ ＊

A definition of a business employee is. . .one who walks into the boss's office with a heluva good idea and when he leaves, the boss has a brilliant one!

＊ ＊ ＊ ＊ ＊

My boss is one cheap guy. He knows he can't take it with him, but he's counting on the resurrection when he can come back and get it.

＊ ＊ ＊ ＊ ＊

How many maintenance men does it take to screw in a lightbulb? Only one to force it with a hammer and six to go out for more lightbulbs.

Old statisticians never die--they just know when their number is up.

✳ ✳ ✳ ✳ ✳

Hard work never hurt or killed anyone. On the other hand, laziness and relaxing never caused any casualties.

✳ ✳ ✳ ✳ ✳

When I advised my tough, master-sergeant-type assistant that one catches more flies with sugar than vinegar, he said, "What the hell would I do with a lot of flies!"

✳ ✳ ✳ ✳ ✳

How would you describe your new boss?
Well, let's see. You could say, after working for him, that stuffed shirts come in all sizes!

✳ ✳ ✳ ✳ ✳

If you have what you want, you're rich. If you can do without it, you're richer.

✳ ✳ ✳ ✳ ✳

Enthusiasm is a concept invented by the young and inexperienced.

✳ ✳ ✳ ✳ ✳

I hated my boss. So did everybody else in the department. He was a true SOB. But one day a hilarious thing happened. The jerk collapsed at work. And do you know what? We summoned the paramedics by mail. . .and Fourth Class at that!

✳ ✳ ✳ ✳ ✳

My boss is one tough geezer. I truly dislike him and he me. I guess that's why we get along like Cain and Abel.

✳ ✳ ✳ ✳ ✳

They advocate gardening for supervisors in my company. They say it's good training for being on their knees.

The boss was taking a group of visitors on a tour of the office and they came to the mailroom. "This is not an efficient operation," the boss said, "nothing ever seems to get right here because of late deliveries, wrong deliveries, non-deliveries." Just then he noticed a young man working furiously but happily at sorting mail. The youngster was singing and whistling and never stopped sorting and delivering mail to the proper slots. The boss signaled to the visitor to follow him and he walked up to the young man and said, "I want to congratulate you on your work, young man."

"It isn't work, Sir. It's fun."

"I admire your attitude. We need more workers in this office with that attitude!" And the letters kept on flying into their slots as the young man said, "Thank you, Sir."

The boss watched a bit longer, then said, "You're first-rate, young fellow. I've never seen mail handled so speedily."

"Heck fire, Sir, this is nothing. Just wait till I learn to read."

✳ ✳ ✳ ✳ ✳

Money sure doesn't talk. . .it just goes without saying!

✳ ✳ ✳ ✳ ✳

Most offices have suggestion boxes offering employees a way to offer suggestions to the company. After much research, it has been determined that the boxes contain three or four useful suggestions, half-a-dozen useless suggestions, a gross of immoral suggestions, and 200 to 300 candy wrappers. Could this last contribution be because the suggestion box is halfway to the wastebasket?

✳ ✳ ✳ ✳ ✳

It's a fact that many love affairs begin in the office: That's where many employees first fall in love with money.

✳ ✳ ✳ ✳ ✳

Charles Lamb disliked office life and was inclined to be uncertain about his office hours at the India House. One day his chief said to him, "Mr. Lamb, recently you've been coming in very late to the office."

"Yes, Sir," replied Lamb, "but you will also notice that I leave early."

By the time his superior had worked that one out, Lamb was gone.

Girl who works for a top automobile executive to a friend: "My boss has a split personality--and I loathe them both."

✳ ✳ ✳ ✳ ✳

The head of an advertising agency was emphasizing to an employee the necessity of high-pressure advertising. "Repetition, repetition is the keynote," he said, pounding the desk. "Harp on your product in every way possible, cram it down people's throats, make yourself sickening if you have to, but don't ever forget to repeat and repeat. It's the only way to get results. Now what was it you wanted to see me about?"

"Well, Sir," answered the employee, "I'd like a raise. A raise! A *raise*! A RAISE!"

✳ ✳ ✳ ✳ ✳

Personnel manager to prospective employee: "Oh, we have our own special type of incentive plan, Mr. Feuer--we fire at the drop of a hat!"

Overheard: "You are looking remarkably cheerful today. Did you win the rat race?"

* * * * *

Employee who received by mistake a pay envelope without a check, to accounting department: "What happened? Did my deductions finally catch up with my salary?"

* * * * *

Personnel man to trainee: "Or if you prefer, you may elect to avoid coffee breaks entirely and retire three years early."

* * * * *

An unemployed guy walked into the office of Peter Wallace, efficiency expert, and asked, "Sir, if I take your course, what will I learn?"
"You'll learn how to get what you deserve."
"To hell with you, Mister!"

* * * * *

Some guys are just born unlucky. The guy who works next to my bench is that kind. Why, if it were raining soup that guy'd be standing there with a fork.

* * * * *

Question of the year: If work is such a beneficial good, how come they have to pay you to do it?

* * * * *

Our auditor was terribly overweight, so he went on a diet that he had heard was a sure thing. He ate only coconut and milk and it worked. Not only did he lose weight but he climbed the flagpole in front of the office in record time every morning.

* * * * *

There's this one cheap guy in our office. He's terrible. The money he gives to needy people can be counted on one missing finger.

The main drawback to enthusiasm is that when you get carried away with it, all too often you have to walk back!

＊ ＊ ＊ ＊ ＊

It is possible that the reason people are living longer today is that when the angel of death calls, he gets an answering machine.

＊ ＊ ＊ ＊ ＊

Occasionally one meets with an employee whose gall is boundless. We have one like that. She took a two-week vacation and then asked for an extra day because she'd missed so many coffee breaks.

＊ ＊ ＊ ＊ ＊

Some guys are just plain bad eggs from the beginning. This one guy in our office is that type of man. They tell me that when he was a kid on the family farm, he hid his grandpa's bedpan in the ice box!

"DO YOU HAVE A SYMPATHY CARD FOR SOMEONE WHOSE HUSBAND HAS RETIRED?"

Eddie Dunkin was working the machine next to his buddy, Pete. Eddie remarked, "Y'know, Pete, me and my wife got us a new apartment."

"Yeah? Great. Did the landlord ask much for it?"

"Ask much. You bet. Already, they've asked five times!"

* * * * *

The executive caught one of his workers in a back closet with a pretty employee. "Explain this," he bellowed.

"Well, Sir," the worker replied, "neither of us like coffee."

* * * * *

Money isn't everything. . .but it's way ahead of whatever is in second place.

* * * * *

This guy had worked for us for about a year and accomplished nothing. Finally, the boss called him in and said, "Emil, you are about as useful to this company as a glass eye at a keyhole."

* * * * *

Mere wealth can't bring us happiness
Nor can it make us glad.
But flakes'll take a chance with it
On being rich and sad.

* * * * *

Don't ever knock the rich because they're the only ones who can give you a job.

* * * * *

Even though he does not a dad-blamed thing, one shouldn't call him lazy 'cause he's always got a load on.

* * * * *

This jerk in our office is absolutely untrustworthy and he's all bent over, too, probably the result of his living up to his ideals.

206

This new guy in our office is impossible to teach. He knows as little about our procedures as when he came to us a year ago. I think he has a sound-proof head.

***** *** *** *** ***

We got a real suck-up in our office. He was following the boss last week when the boss suddenly stopped and the guy suffered a broken nose.

***** *** *** *** ***

He's a real sourpuss and everybody in the office stays clear of him. You know the kind. . .always seeing germs in the milk of human kindness.

***** *** *** *** ***

Making money was never a problem with me, but. . .trying to pass it is another story.

"WHENEVER THEY TALK ABOUT BEING ON THE CUTTING EDGE, IT MEANS THEY'RE CUTTING SALARIES AGAIN."

Money doesn't mean a derned thing. I'm positive that a guy who has one hundred million bucks isn't a bit happier than a guy with ninety million.

* * * * *

My buddy in the shop just bought his mother-in-law a chair. But she refuses to let him plug it in!

* * * * *

You know you are properly motivated when your dreams show you in work clothes.

* * * * *

It was an all-women corporation but they had some heavy work to do and decided there was no alternative to hiring a man. The first applicant was asked to hoist a hundred-pound sack and he did. Then he was asked to pull down to the floor an inordinately heavy box of books. He did. Satisfied, the interrogatress asked to see his testimonials. "Lady," he replied, "I'll do anything you want but I ain't gonna show you my testimonials!"

* * * * *

I'm beginning to get furious with my boss because every time I come in early, he asks: "Having trouble at home?"

* * * * *

Too many of our guys just kill too much time. It wouldn't be so bad if they'd *work* it to death, but they don't.

* * * * *

Wesley Bass was up in years and still working hard every day. One of his buddies advised him to eat more natural food but he shook his head negating the suggestion, saying, "I need all the preservatives I can get."

* * * * *

To make a long story short, there's nothing that'll do it like the supervisor walking in.

A guy applied for a job and asked about the benefits. The personnel manager explained about medical insurance, saying the premium would be deducted from his paycheck. The applicant said: "That's not so good. In my last company, they paid for my insurance policy, gave me a month's sick leave and one year's severance pay. They also gave us bonuses throughout the years. Our day's work ended at three PM and I got a cup of coffee anything I wanted it. We all got all those perks."

"Then I don't understand," the personnel manager said, "why did you quit such a great job?"

"They went broke," the applicant replied.

✳ ✳ ✳ ✳ ✳

The personnel manager and his assistant were discussing the need to hire a new receptionist. "It shouldn't be a hard job at all," the manager said. "Even if she knows little, we can teach her what's right and what's wrong."

"Yes, Sir! Right!" the assistant said, nodding, "Yes, Sir, you teach her what's right!"

✳ ✳ ✳ ✳ ✳

The young man applied for a job and presented his resume that read: "I am a Yale graduate who refused to take a vice-presidency of a major steel fence company and I never ask about salary because I don't care about money. The clock doesn't exist for me and I don't care how many hours a week I must work."

The personnel manager asked: "Don't you have even one normal human weakness?"

"My buddies all say I fib a little."

✳ ✳ ✳ ✳ ✳

A fellow applied for a job and gave several fine references, one from his minister and several from elders in his church. The personnel manager, who looked over his application, said: "These are fine but could you give me references from someone who knows you weekdays!"

Our personnel officer says that honesty comes from training background, religious instruction, and. . .fear of getting caught.

✳ ✳ ✳ ✳ ✳

My friend's daughter just graduated from college and applied for her first job. Under "sex" she wrote, "Just try it."

✳ ✳ ✳ ✳ ✳

Johnny Desmond came home looking forlorn. He staggered into the house and his wife asked: "Johnny, how come you look so beat-up and dismal?"

"It's the boss," Johnny replied. "He gave me a unique order: 'Get out! Stay out! And don't come back!'"

"IT'S A SUIT FOR A MAN ON HIS WAY UP."

If your boss is grim and yet you must ask him for a raise, you'll be surprised at how your request will change his expression from grim to laughing out loud!

* * * * *

It had been the first season since the Depression that the Sinclair Iron and Metal Corporation had had a loss, a catastrophic loss. The boss walked into his office the morning after he'd received the terrible statement on his business and shouted: "How come nobody in this company is working?"

"That's easy, boss," a voice answered. "This time you're wearing rubber heels!"

* * * * *

He had an office so tiny that one inch smaller and it would have been adultery!
Dorothy Parker

* * * * *

Tom Stevens worked as a salesclerk in the town's largest department store. He was on his lunch hour when he met an old friend who used to work with him in the same department.

"What are you doing now, Joe?" Tom asked his friend.

"I'm a cop. Went through the academy and now sport a billy club and a gun. Off duty today."

"Is it a good job? Do you enjoy the work?"

"Swell job. And what's really great about the work is that the customer is always wrong!"

* * * * *

Our supervisor has a great reputation, absolutely unwarranted. My boss sent him to Washington to fill one of those dollar-a-year jobs, and they sent him home, claimed he was overpaid!

* * * * *

Retirement at sixty-five is ridiculous. When I was sixty-five, I still had pimples.
George Burns

"Mary Jo, how long have you worked here?" an employee asked.

"Let me put it this way," Mary Jo replied. "I've worked here ever since my boss threatened to fire me."

✳ ✳ ✳ ✳ ✳

An honest appraisal of his income and the spending of it, by Errol Flynn, the movie actor: "My trouble lies in reconciling my gross habits with my net income."

✳ ✳ ✳ ✳ ✳

My boss is one of those ultra pious guys. A few years ago, he claims that he took a walk and was hit by a motor boat!

✳ ✳ ✳ ✳ ✳

"There were times that my pants were so thin, I could sit on a dime and tell whether it was heads or tails."
Spencer Tracy

✳ ✳ ✳ ✳ ✳

John Gill, the young man just hired to assist the boss, walked into the boss's office and said, "Sir, my wife is having a baby and I'd appreciate it if you could give me the afternoon off."

"Certainly, John. by all means take it off and good luck."

The next day, Johnny was at work at his desk and the boss walked up to him, saying, "I guess congratulations are in order and did you have a boy or girl?"

"It's a bit premature to tell, Sir, because we'll have to wait nine months to know."

✳ ✳ ✳ ✳ ✳

That money talks
I'll not deny.
I heard it once;
It said "Good-bye."

"Those who will follow blindly on <u>this</u> side, and those who will swallow blame on <u>this</u> side. We're separating the sheep from the scapegoats."

© 1993 Jonny Hawkins

Sympathy is defined as what you give your buddy when you don't want to give him money!

* * * * *

George met his friend, Basil, after a two-week vacation. Basil asked him how he enjoyed his two weeks and George said, "A friend allowed me two weeks in his fishing and hunting camp up in Minnesota. No night life, no booze, no gambling and no women."
"Did you have a great time?"
"Who went?"

* * * * *

Some guys simply don't know the how or what or why or means of making it in today's world. When opportunity knocks at their door, they're out in back looking for four-leaf clovers!

The brain is a wonderful organ; it starts working the moment you get up in the morning and doesn't stop until you get to the office.

Robert Frost

✳ ✳ ✳ ✳ ✳

The office manager had suspected an employee of dishonesty for a long time. The reason? The girl lived in an expensive apartment in Detroit, drove to work in a Bentley, and entertained lavishly both friends and fellow employees in her office. So, one day, he asked her: "Maybelle, you make $500 a month here and I know that you live a higher style of life than the president of our company. Where do you get the money to live as you do?"

Maybelle explained: "You see, each week I raffle a couple of thousand raffle tickets to friends and other folks in the office here. I sell each ticket for $2.00."

"Oh. . .you work a raffle, eh? What do you raffle off?"

"My paycheck!"

✳ ✳ ✳ ✳ ✳

I am a friend of the working man and I would rather be a friend than be one.

Clarence Darrow

✳ ✳ ✳ ✳ ✳

The worker had just won a four-million-dollar settlement from his company for a crippling injury suffered at work. He claimed absolute incapacity to use his legs. The company tried to prove the guy was lying but seeing him in court, with his wife and kids, swayed the jury and they awarded him a the huge settlement.

When the worker came to the insurance company to get his check, he was met with a phalanx of furious executives and lawyers of the company. "We're going to follow you day and night, every place you go, take photos of you all the time and as soon as we get evidence that you were lying and can walk normally, we'll have you back in court. Here's your check. And just what are you going to do with all this money?"

"Well, gentlemen," the cripple said. "My wife and I and the kids are going to Europe. We've always wanted to see Paris,

Barcelona, Prague, London and then we'll go to the shrine at Lourdes. And it is there, Gentlemen, that the world will see the greatest miracle since the time of Jesus!"

✳ ✳ ✳ ✳ ✳ ✳

Our office manager is an awful braggart and a real pain. We got even with him the other day when he announced to our office that his wife was pregnant. Someone yelled: "Who do you suspect?"

✳ ✳ ✳ ✳ ✳ ✳

A certain labor consultant came to the conclusion that work is the most unpopular way to make a living.

✳ ✳ ✳ ✳ ✳ ✳

This friend of mine, who works next to me, has become the nation's topmost worrier. I'm sure of it. Y'know why? He's got a note from the bank and a lovely girlfriend and both. . .both are overdue.

✳ ✳ ✳ ✳ ✳ ✳

My boss's mind is like concrete. . .all mixed up and permanently set!

✳ ✳ ✳ ✳ ✳ ✳

Be sure to work eight hours and sleep eight hours but...not the same eight hours.

✳ ✳ ✳ ✳ ✳ ✳

This corporation requires no exercise programs because everyone gets sufficient exercise jumping to conclusions, flying off the handle, running down the boss, knifing friends behind the back, dodging responsibility and pushing their luck.

✳ ✳ ✳ ✳ ✳ ✳

Those who believe that the dead never return to life...should be here at quitting time.

Sign near a fire exit:
IN CASE OF FIRE: Simply flee building with the same reckless abandon that occurs each day at quitting time.

* * * * *

Nothing is impossible for the man who doesn't have to do it himself.

* * * * *

"Who's the new guy in the office?"
"I don't know his name but he's a C.P.N."
"I think you mean C.P.A., don't you?"
"No, C.P.N.--Constant Pain in the Neck."

"SOMETHING TELLS ME WE SHOULD HAVE SEEN THIS COMING."

An assistant to the office manager was sent to the office supply store to get a typewriter. He arrived there and asked them about their product. When he found one he liked, he said to the store manager: "I understand that my company has owed you for three years for our last typewriter. That right?"

"It sure is. Are you ready to pay up now?"

The customer said, "Afraid not, but we would like to buy another one, like this one, for the same terms."

✳ ✳ ✳ ✳ ✳

It's difficult to soar with eagles when you work with turkeys.

✳ ✳ ✳ ✳ ✳

Two accountants heard of the death of a friend. They went to the cemetery to pay homage at his grave but they could not locate it. They looked and looked and finally one said, "Do you think I might have put it in his wife's name?"

✳ ✳ ✳ ✳ ✳

Be like a duck. . .above water, stay cool and calm but below water, paddle like hell!

✳ ✳ ✳ ✳ ✳

The company's new accountant had a peculiar habit. Every morning, when he arrived at his desk, he would open the second drawer, remove a folded piece of paper, open it, read it, then return it to the drawer. The manager was curious as to why he did this, so, one morning, early, before the man had arrived, he opened the desk drawer and took out the folded paper and this is what it said: "The credit side is the one nearest the door."

✳ ✳ ✳ ✳ ✳

My father taught me to work He did not teach me to love it.
            Abraham Lincoln

We had to let go a long-time bookkeeper of ours because our new computer did everything he had done. The poor guy. And what made it worse is that his wife went out and bought the exact kind of computer!

✻ ✻ ✻ ✻ ✻

One of the happiest songs in tribute to money is: "Abide with Me."

✻ ✻ ✻ ✻ ✻

"I had a terrible experience the other day," the boss told his stenographer. "I went to a new stockbroker and asked about a certain stock. . .IBM. This guy turned to his notebook and asked: "How do you spell it?"

From *Nothing Serious - Just A Little Chat With The Boss*
Reprinted by permission of Ann E. Weeks, DNS
Passage Publishing, Inc. - Louisville, KY

Be awful nice to 'em goin' up, because you're gonna meet 'em all comin' down.
Jimmy Durante

✳ ✳ ✳ ✳ ✳

Work has a main factor that much resembles yeast. . .like yeast, it raises the dough.

✳ ✳ ✳ ✳ ✳

We figured a perfect budget in our business. The money we owe figures to the exact last penny, the same as the money we spent.

✳ ✳ ✳ ✳ ✳

Our accountant is just too sharp to be real. He's so wise they named a loophole after him.

✳ ✳ ✳ ✳ ✳

"I consider Johnny Edwards a first-rate druggist."
"I agree. But I do think he makes his chicken salad a little too greasy!"

✳ ✳ ✳ ✳ ✳

To err is human. To *really* foul things up requires a computer!

✳ ✳ ✳ ✳ ✳

In the boxing match that is existence, talent is the punch; tact is the clever footwork.
Wilson Mizner

✳ ✳ ✳ ✳ ✳

"I get a nice salary. . .it runs into six figures."
"That's nice. Is it adequate?"
"Not really. Y'see, the six figures are. . .my wife and five kids!"

A fellow who's bald-headed is a guy who came out on top.

* * * * *

Stan was an accountant in our firm and his one problem was getting along with the women in our office. As he put it one day: "It's time the girls in this office came to the conclusion that they are men's equals. In the past, they always thought they were superior!"

* * * * *

A Chicago company was hiring a new accountant and had asked three of them to appear for an interview. The first one was called in and asked: "How much is four plus four?" The answer was: "Eight." "Right."

The next applicant was asked the same question and replied: "Eight point zero."

"Thank you and that is all," said the reviewer and called in the third applicant. "How much is four plus four?" was the question.

"Tell me," the applicant replied, "just how much do you want it to be?"

They hired the third applicant!

* * * * *

Don't steal: Thou'lt never thus compete successfully in business. Cheat!
Ambrose Pierce

* * * * *

A verbal contract isn't worth the paper it's written on.
Samuel Goldwyn

* * * * *

A good definition of your expert in income taxes is this: "An efficient accountant in income tax counseling and preparation is one whose fee is the total amount that you saved in your final income tax submittal."

We just lost our company accountant. He was just too shy for the job. What do I mean, shy? Well, he was shy a quarter of a million dollars!

※ ※ ※ ※ ※

Our accountant says that honesty pays. "Probably does," one employee responded. "But it doesn't pay enough!"

※ ※ ※ ※ ※

One reason honesty is the best policy and so successful is that it has so little competition.

※ ※ ※ ※ ※

Did you hear about the two computers--one male, the other female--that·met at the computer show? Well, the female computer offered the male an Apple. The male asked, "Is your name Eve?"

※ ※ ※ ※ ※

Currency: A material that isn't current enough!

※ ※ ※ ※ ※

An experienced corporate executive once described a corporate optimist as an executive who married his secretary under the conviction that he could go on dictating to her.

※ ※ ※ ※ ※

"How's the banking business this week, Sam?"
"Much better. I'm looking for a new cashier."
"But I thought you hired one last week?"
"I did. He's the one I'm looking for."

※ ※ ※ ※ ※

Let us all be happy and live within our means. . .even if we have to borrow to do it.
                    Artemus Ward

If you would know the value of money, go try to borrow some; for he that goes a-borrowing goes a-sorrowing.
Ben Franklin

✳ ✳ ✳ ✳ ✳

"Susie, don't you have an uncle who is an artist?"
"Well, if you want to call him that...he draws welfare!"

✳ ✳ ✳ ✳ ✳

A statistician is a technician who comes to the rescue of figures that can't lie for themselves.

✳ ✳ ✳ ✳ ✳

Statistics show that there are only three ages when men are sinful: young, old and middle.

"EXACTLY HOW LONG HAVE YOU BEEN IN THE UNEMPLOYMENT LINE?"

HOW YOU CAN TELL WHEN IT'S GOING TO BE A ROTTEN DAY

You wake up face down on the pavement.

You put your bra on backward and it fits better.

You call Suicide Prevention and they put you on hold.

You see a "60 Minutes" news team waiting in your office.

Your birthday cake collapses from the weight of the candles.

Your son tells you he wishes Anita Bryant (singer who waged a one-woman campaign against homosexuality) should mind her own business.

You want to put on the clothes you wore home from the party and there aren't any.

You turn on the news and they're showing emergency routes out of the city.

Your twin sister forgot your birthday.

You wake up and discover your waterbed broke and then realize that you don't have a waterbed.

Your car horn goes off accidentally and remains stuck as you follow a group of Hell's Angles on the freeway.

Your wife wakes up feeling amorous and you have a headache.

Your boss tells you not to bother to take off your coat.

The bird singing outside your window is a buzzard.

You wake up and your braces are locked together.

You walk to work and find your dress is stuck in the back of your pantyhose.

You call your answering service and they tell you it's none of your business.

Your blind date turns out to be your ex-wife.

Your income tax check bounces.

You put both contact lenses in the same eye.

Your pet rock snaps at you.

Your wife says, "Good morning, Bill" and your name is George.

When You're Up to Your Ass in Alligators
by Alan Dundes and Carl R. Pagter
Wayne State University Press
Detroit, MI: 1987

It has often been noted that success is relative. The more you have of it, the more relatives you have.

✳ ✳ ✳ ✳ ✳

A young fellow graduated from Yale University and went to work for a huge international corporation. He worked hard and diligently for several months without notice, promotion, or raise in pay. About a year after starting work, he was called into the president's office.

"You've been here a year, now," the president said. "Have you been getting any notice or encouragement or attention of any sort?"

"Sir, it's as if I didn't work here. Nobody notices me."

"Well," the president said, "I'm promoting you to vice-president and increasing your salary by fifty thousand dollars a year."

"Wonderful," the young man responded. "I'm eternally grateful."

"Is that all you've got to say?" asked the president.

"Well. . .well. . .I sure do thank you, Dad!"

"No, no, a thousand times no, your health package does not include hair loss treatments."

Imagination is the most important quality of a copywriter. And if you want proof, just take a look at my expense account.

※ ※ ※ ※ ※

The office manager was overtaken with patriotic fervor and placed American flags all over the building, in every office, and even in the restrooms. Some time later, a lady approached him and asked that the flag in the ladies restroom be removed.

"Certainly not," responded the manager. "Have you no patriotic feelings, no love of liberty?"

"Yes we do, Sir. That's the trouble. We have a hard time facing the flag sitting down."

※ ※ ※ ※ ※

Nothing astonishes men so much as common sense and plain dealing.
Ralph Waldo Emerson

※ ※ ※ ※ ※

"I'll never retire because there isn't a thing I can't do now that I didn't do at 18. . .and that gives you an idea of how pathetic I was at 18."

※ ※ ※ ※ ※

Boss: "Boy, how long does it take you to get to work in this office?"
Employee: "About one hour after I get here."

※ ※ ※ ※ ※

Boss (furious): "Mr. Peters, do you know what time we start work in this office?"
Peters: "I'm not sure of that because whenever I get here the rest of the employees are already working."

※ ※ ※ ※ ※

"How many people work in your office?"
"I'd say. . .about half."

YOU KNOW IT'S A ROUGH DAY WHEN. . .

You drive into the repair shop, and your mechanic starts singing, "I'm in the Money."

The deduction from the raise you just got is so big that you have to take a second job to replace the money you lost.

You tell the salesclerk you are looking for a potholder and she directs you to the girdle department.

You are contemplating lining the rim of your boss's coffee cup with Super Glue.

The Steve Wilson Report
Steve Wilson & Co.
344 South Merkle Road
Bexley, OH 43209-1820

❋ ❋ ❋ ❋ ❋

Here are Mark Twain's comments on human values:
In Boston, they ask, "How much does he know?"
In New York, they ask, "How much is he worth?"
In Philadelphia, "Who were his parents?"

YES, WE DO HAVE MANY OPPORTUNITIES FOR ADVANCEMENT HERE.

Brown: "I hear the boss fired you for lying. Is that true?"
Black: "Yep. He fired me for lying in bed for an hour too long every morning."

* * * * *

"I take it you're looking for work?"
"Not necessarily. . .what I want is a job."

* * * * *

Computers aren't so new. Didn't Adam have an Apple II?
G. K., Edwardsville, IL

* * * * *

THE RICH MAN

The rich man has his motorcar,
    His country and his town estate.
He smokes a fifty-cent cigar
    And jeers at fate.

He frivols through the livelong day,
    He knows not poverty her pinch.
His lot seems light, his heart seems gay,
    He has a cinch.

Yet though my lamp burns low and dim,
    Though I must slave for livelihood--
Think you that I would change with him?
    You Bet I Would!

* * * * *

Selma Smothers was a bookkeeper with the Altruna Blouse Company. One evening, after work, she'd been shopping and was loaded with packages. She stood waiting for the bus door to open and, when it did, found that she was so loaded that, with her tight dress, she could not mount the bus stairs. She reached back to unzip her dress a bit hoping that would help. It didn't. So, she reached back again and zipped down the dress even further. No good. Finally, a young man, standing in the line impatient to get on the bus, picked her up and carried her up the steps to the pay station. "How dare you, a stranger, do this to me?" Selma shrieked.

"Well, you see," the young man began to explain, "after you zipped down my pants zipper the second time, I thought we'd become darned good friends!"

✳ ✳ ✳ ✳ ✳

Unlike business, strip poker is the game in which the more you lose, the more you can show for it.

✳ ✳ ✳ ✳ ✳

Experience: The satisfying knowledge that allows you to recognize a mistake when you make it again.

✳ ✳ ✳ ✳ ✳

After working late one night, Paul Povse left the office and started for home down a dark side street. Suddenly, a voice came out of the darkness: "Sir, could you please help a poor man out with a few bucks? I'm at the end of the rope and all I have left is this gun!"

✳ ✳ ✳ ✳ ✳

It seems only fair to credit Adam and Eve with being the first bookkeepers. After all, it was they who invented the loose-leaf system.

✳ ✳ ✳ ✳ ✳

Nevur wurk befor brakfust. If yu hav tu wurk befor brakfust, git yur brakfust fust.
Josh Billings

✳ ✳ ✳ ✳ ✳

He had insomnia so bad that he couldn't sleep while working.
Arthur "Bugs" Baer

✳ ✳ ✳ ✳ ✳

Work is the greatest thing in the world. So we should save some of it for tomorrow.
Don Herold

"It gives me great pleasure to present you with the 'Jerk At Work' award for this month."

✳ ✳ ✳ ✳ ✳

I like work. It fascinates me. I can sit and look at it for hours.
>Jerome K. Jerome

✳ ✳ ✳ ✳ ✳

It is impossible to enjoy idling. . .unless one has plenty of work to do.
>Jerome K. Jerome

✳ ✳ ✳ ✳ ✳

I am a great believer in luck. And I find that the harder I work the more I have of it.
>Stephen Leacock

I go on working for the same reason a hen goes on laying eggs.
H. L. Mencken

* * * * *

What is essential to do is worth the trouble of asking somebody to do it!

* * * * *

If you don't succeed at first, you'll get a lot of advice.

* * * * *

If you practice "early to bed, early to rise," work late, and pay your taxes, you surely will get ahead. . .providing you strike oil!

* * * * *

Talk about your workaholic. . .Eddie Brown said he loved Christmas because nobody bothered him at the office.

* * * * *

A new idea is much like a child. . .easier conceived than delivered.

* * * * *

The man who fails to blow his own horn is doomed never to hear the sound of music.

* * * * *

The trouble with the rat race is that even if you win, you're still a rat.
Mark Twain

* * * * *

It is said that a lie is an abomination before the Lord, but sure as heck is an ever-present help in time of trouble.

Here's a story to illustrate today's major problem...personal debt:

"How do you spend your income?" the boss asked his assistant.

"Thirty percent goes for payment on my home, thirty percent goes for clothes for all six of us. Forty percent goes for food and we spend twenty percent for entertainment."

"But all that adds up to 120%."

"That's right."

✳ ✳ ✳ ✳ ✳

"Tell me, how did Bud Smith make all that money?"

"He invested judiciously and speculated even more carefully."

"Is that so? Well, tell me this. . .how did Paul Barker lose all his money?"

"By gambling on the stock market!"

"BIDWELL, YOU'RE FIRED! DISMISSED! DISCHARGED! FINISHED! TERMINATED..."

Did you hear about Roland Pearson, the most efficient, most respected efficiency expert on the east coast? Well, he died and was being taken to his grave by eight men bearing the coffin. Suddenly the coffin opened and the expert sat up. "Do you realize," he shouted, "that if you'd put my coffin on wheels, you could lay off four guys!"

✻ ✻ ✻ ✻ ✻

Inflation: What used to cost $100 to buy, now costs $200 to repair.

✻ ✻ ✻ ✻

Two old men were discussing the 1929 stock market crash. One of them said: "We were well off until 1929, when we lost everything."

"Your father must have been a big banker or producer of some sort, right?"

"No, not really. He had a newspaper stand."

"Really? And how could a stock market crash hurt him?"

"After the crash, some guy jumped out of the twentieth floor of the Patterson Building and smashed into his stand. We lost everything!"

✻ ✻ ✻ ✻ ✻

They say that this sign drove off a lot of job-seekers:

"If you consider that work is a real pleasure, you can have loads of fun around here."

✻ ✻ ✻ ✻ ✻

Eddie Roberts was a small-town boy who had come to the big city and become rich. He was telling a friend of his background. "When I came to this city, I had only three dollars to my name. But I didn't go around whining about poverty. No sir."

"Obviously," the friend said, "you must have invested that three bucks wisely."

"I sure as hell did. . .I spent it for a wire to my father for more dough."

In the personnel office of a major U.S. corporation, they posted this sign:
YOUR SALARY RAISE WILL BE EFFECTIVE WHEN YOU ARE.

＊ ＊ ＊ ＊ ＊

It's a study in contradictions that every year it takes less time to fly across the ocean and more time to drive to work!

＊ ＊ ＊ ＊ ＊

"Share the wealth, I believe in that," one office employee said to his fellow worker. "I believe we should all divide our wealth with another person."

"Great idea. I agree," replied his friend. "If you had two thousand bucks, would you give me half?"

"Yer darn tootin' I would."

"And if you had two Cadillacs, would you give me one of 'em?"

"You bet I would!"

"And if you had only two shirts, would you give me one of 'em?"

"Nope, I sure as heck wouldn't."

"But why not?"

"Because. . .well. . .y'see. . .I've got two shirts!"

＊ ＊ ＊ ＊ ＊

"What advantage do I get if I join the union?" the new employee asked.

"Well, there are plenty," replied the union executive. "When you die, all payments to the union cease."

＊ ＊ ＊ ＊ ＊

A laborer discovered that he was one dollar short in his pay envelope. He complained to the cashier, who looked at the record and said: "We paid you a buck too much last week. You didn't even mention it then, did you!"

"Look, Sister. . .an occasional mistake, I can overlook, but this makes two in a row!"

A hot discussion was going on relative to the election procedures in the union. There was no agreement as to the honesty of the elections and appeared to be no majority one way or the other until one guy spoke up: "Don't tell me the elections are crooked! I know they are. Why, in our last election, I ran for shop steward of this local and I voted for myself three times and still I never got a single vote when they counted them!"

❈ ❈ ❈ ❈ ❈

They tell this story about a labor leader who went to a matrimonial agency. "Tell me," he said to the head of the agency, "Is this a union enterprise?"

"It sure is," the boss assured him.

"In that case, I'll take this scrumptious brunette," the union leader said, after seeing the twenty-year-old beauty's photo.

"No, you've got to take this lady," the manager said, showing a photo of a 60-year-old woman.

"Why? What do you mean? Why her?" screamed the union leader.

"Because she has seniority!"

SORRY, BOYS, BUT TECHNOLOGY HAS REDUCED MY
DEMAND FOR MANUAL LABOR.

All applicants for a job at a proposed hydroelectric plant in Tennessee had to take a written examination. When one applicant read the first question: "Give the meaning of hydroelectric," he wrote, "It means I don't get the job."

$$* * * * *$$

A young woman applied for a job at an east coast munitions factory and struggled over the final question on the application: "What are your hopes, aims, ambitions?" She thought for quite a while, then wrote: "I hope to go as far as my education, talent, and sex will allow."

$$* * * * *$$

I was playing golf in Wyoming when suddenly I saw a rattlesnake, the first I'd seen in a long time. "Be careful!" I warned my three buddies of the foursome. "Don't get too close or it'll strike!"

"Holy smokes," one of them replied. "Do those critters have unions, too?"

$$* * * * *$$

A retired union veteran grew bored doing nothing and applied for a job. "How many years experience do you have?" the prospective employer asked.

"Sixty," was the reply.

"What! How could you have sixty years experience when you're only fifty-nine years old?"

"Easy," the man replied. "I put in one heluva lot of overtime!"

$$* * * * *$$

The union's negotiator had won a great contract for the men in negotiations with the company six months before. Now, he was back wanting to negotiate once again. The company's negotiator said, "In the last round, you got your wage demand plus three coffee breaks, hospitalization for parents and grandparents, vacations, birthdays off. . .so now what the hell is it you want?"

"Only one thing," the union negotiator said, "just a guarantee that you won't go broke."

Samuel Gompers, the great American labor movement's chief, was once asked just what it was that the unions wanted. His response was direct and honest. He replied: "More!"

* * * * *

Did you know how a union leader begins a fairy tale to his child at bedtime? He begins. . ."Once upon a time-and-a-half. . ."

* * * * *

The union was picketing a showing of a violent thriller but the picket line was ineffective. So the union held a conference and decided to change tactics. They put three men out to picket, each carrying a sign that read: "The hero's brother-in-law did it."

* * * * *

Spitzer, the union honcho, walked out of the conference room of the Made Rite Shirt Company. It had been a difficult week of negotiations but an agreement had been reached. He now stood before a gathering of workers, saying: "Here is what we agreed to, men." The union official said. "If you have seniority, you get $40,000 a year along with free medical service and retirement at age 46. Your car insurance is paid for with free parking for your car. Your kids get their college tuition paid for and you only work on Mondays."

"Hey, Spitzer," a union member called out, "Is that every Monday?"

* * * * *

It seems as though union activists are always at management's throat. Probably that's because it keeps them away from the other place that management expects them to kiss.

* * * * *

A union leader died and found himself standing before the Pearly Gates. St. Peter asked: 'Well, don't just stand there. Make up your mind. Do you or do you not wish to enter?"

The union official just stood there watching an endless line of angels pass back and forth in front of him. The union official shook his head. "I ain't comin' in," he said. "I ain't never crossed a picket line and I sure as hell don't mean to do it now!"

✳ ✳ ✳ ✳ ✳

The head of our company had refused to sign the new contract with the union. Two union reps came to visit him but could not talk him into signing the agreement. So they resorted to violence, hitting him in the face, the belly, and the groin until the boss collapsed on the floor! Still laying there, the union guys presented, once again, their contract for signature and the boss signed it. "Good! Finally!" the union guys said. "How come you didn't sign it before?"

"Because you guys didn't explain it properly," the boss replied.

"We're all concerned about the nuclear threat Hodges. But until the big boom, would you mind doing a little something around here?"

7

STOCKS and BROKERS

October is one of the particularly dangerous months to speculate in stocks. The others are July, January, September, April, November, May, March, June, December, August, and January.
Mark Twain

✳ ✳ ✳ ✳ ✳

George Enos, a stockbroker, was vacationing in Florida when he became deathly ill. He was rushed to the hospital and became unconscious enroute. He came out of his coma in the hospital just as a nurse was removing a thermometer. "Have I got a temperature, nurse?" he asked.

"Yes you do," said the nurse. "It's a hundred and three."

"Not so bad," the patient said. "When it gets to one hundred and four, sell."

"IT MUST BE THE STOCK BROKERAGE."

"My friend, Eddie, just made a killing in the stock market."
"Yeah? Everybody else lost money. How'd he do it?"
"Shot his broker!"

✳ ✳ ✳ ✳ ✳

Rule No. 1
The Customer Is Always Right

Rule No. 2
If the Customer Is Wrong, Refer to Rule No. 1

✳ ✳ ✳ ✳ ✳

For the benefit of those who contemplate investing in stocks, we append the following list of well-known securities, together with an explanatory index of what each represents:

CERTAIN STOCKS, AND THEIR SIGNIFICANCE

American Spirits	Yankee Cheerfulness
American Surety	The United States Constitution
American Brass	Proverbial Yankee Cheek
Bald Butte	The American Eagle
Boston Elevated	Beacon Hill
Corn Products	Aching Feet
Copper Range	The Policeman's Beat
Hocking Valley	The Manservant who Pawns Things
Majestic Copper	The Average Bluecoat
Old Colony	Home for Aged Couples
Pacific Mail	A Peaceful Quaker
Pump Preferred	The Pretty Female Reporter
Pacific Mills	Friendly Boxing Bouts
People's Gas	Congressional Speeches
Pullman	The City Hall Grafter
Paper Preferred	Crisp Greenbacks
Rubber Goods	Turkish Toweling
Rubber Common	The Advertising Massage Artist
Rubber Preferred	One You Win at Whist
Standard Coupler	The Clergyman
Swift Packing	The Jam on the Elevated
Singer Manufacturing Co	Conservatory of Music
Standard Rope	The Venerable Gold Brick Swindle
United States Steel	The Post-Office Frauds

Union Pacific	. . . .	A Happy Marriage
Union Terminal	. . . .	The Divorce Court
United Fruit	. . . .	A Bunch of Bananas
Wheeling Preferred	. . . .	The Auto Fad at Present
Western Union	. . . .	A Mormon Marriage
Yarn Preferred	. . . .	One that's New

Foolish Finance
Compiled by Gideon Wurdz
John Luce & Co., Publishers
Boston, MA: 1904

✳ ✳ ✳ ✳ ✳

Do you know why they call these guys, "brokers"? Because every time you listen to them and take their advice, that's what you are.

"WHEN DO YOU THINK YOUR DECLINE STARTED?"

The investor called his stockbroker but was told the guy was busy on the phone with his wife.

"Well, tell me," the caller asked, "today, is he bullish or bearish?"

"He's on the phone with his wife. Therefore, he's sheepish."

* * * * *

It had been one of the worst years ever in Tal Johannson's tool business. He called his secretary in and said, "Please get my broker on the phone!"

"Certainly, Sir," she said. "Do I call stock or pawn?"

* * * * *

After the last terrible dip in the stock market, they call the firm. . .OW JONES!

* * * * *

Don't try to buy at the bottom and sell at the top. That can't be done. . .except by liars.
Bernard Baruch

"IT WAS A ROLLER-COASTER DAY ON WALL STREET, WITH STOCKS FALLING 175 FEET TO THEIR DEATH."

Bulls can make money and bears can make money but hogs just get slaughtered.
Wall Street Adage

✳ ✳ ✳ ✳ ✳

There are two times in a man's life when he shouldn't speculate: When he can afford it and when he can't.
Mark Twain

✳ ✳ ✳ ✳ ✳

It had been a hectic day on the stock market and Pete, a stockbroker, was exhausted. He didn't feel up to a long ride home in the suburbs. So he went to a nearby hotel and asked the clerk for a room for the night.

"Very well, Sir," the desk clerk said. "Do you want a room for sleeping or jumping?"

"THEY'RE LAST YEAR'S COMPUTERS."

The leading philosopher of the New York Stock Exchange was heard remarking about the new styles in ladies bathing suits. "We'd better all of us start laughing at these diminutive garments," he said, "because if things keep on this way, there'll be nothing to laugh at."

✳ ✳ ✳ ✳ ✳

ADVICE TO A STOCKHOLDER

Similar in tone to the earlier item is the following standard letter presumably to be sent to corporate stockholders. Actually, this example could be considered a traditional letter. it has been included here because of its utilization of the double-entendre technique. It was popular in the early 1950's.

Dear Stockholder:

Our attention has been called to the fact that you are holding stock in the following corporations:

American Can Company
United Gas & Water Company
Consolidated Water Works

Because of current conditions, we would advise you to sit tight on your American Can, let your Gas go, and hold your Water.

Also you may be interested to know that Scots Tissue touched a new bottom today and that thousands have been wiped clean.

Yours truly,

I. P. Daily
United Brokers Association

Work Hard and You Shall Be Rewarded,
by Alan Dundes and Carl R. Pagter
Reprinted with permission of:
Wayne State University Press,
Detroit, MI 48201-1309

© 1994 Jonny Hawkins

One way to tell when times are good for Wall Street brokers is to look at the ledge of the roof of the stock exchange building. When there are more pigeons than brokers, you know times are good.

✻ ✻ ✻ ✻ ✻

Talk about greedy! On Wall Street, outside the stock exchange, they have a beggar with two hats.

✻ ✻ ✻ ✻ ✻

It is hard to get old habits out of a man. Witness the stockbroker who went to prison where he arranged for the merger of the dining room with the laundry!

"YOUR ASSIGNMENT IS to CONVINCE THE PUBLIC THAT GREED IS A VIRTUE."

Back in 1904, a slender volume of prose–*Foolish Finance*–appeared. It discussed phases of finance (90 years ago!) that pertain just as humorously to the market mystique today, as back in those good old days–the stock exchange, stock speculation, the investor and the broker. Here they are–almost 100 years ago!

THE INVESTOR

The Investor is the System's meal ticket, to be punched full of holes by the Broker as long as there's room on the Margin.

Anybody can be an Investor who has the simple trustfulness of a child and a calling acquaintance at the Bank.

An Investor should also have an iron Constitution and a gold-bearing Declaration of Independence.

He must be quick at reading quotations, quicker at writing checks, and do sums in mental arithmetic at the Board, without the aid of a pointer, with, or without a tip.

He must know the Long and the Short of the game, run to cover faster than a March hare, carry a whole block for many days, unload it all in thirty seconds, hold the market without getting cold feet, make a good delivery in a bad corner, and stand ready to be soaked by the drops that may come from a busted pool.

The Investor must learn to greet Dame Fortune with a frown and Miss Fortune with a smile, and recognize Ruin with quiet dignity when he meets him on The Street. In short, he must carry a poker face and a bottomless purse whenever he strolls through the green fields and beside the distilled waters of Mammon.

The Investor must be the philanthropist-farmer of The Street. His hand must make two margins grow where but one grew before, thus causing the Market to blossom as the rose. For the Promoter may plant and The System water, but the Investor alone giveth the Increase.

The Stock Exchange is his shrine and the Bucket Shop his nursery. Here the Board is spread like a sheet of sticky fly-paper. The busy little Investors hover over it a while, then pick out a fair, smooth spot, put their foot in it, are promptly stuck, and surrender their pretty little greenbacks with the last expiring buzz of the buncoed.

THE BROKER

The Broker is the man who assists the man who assists the

Investor in going broke gracefully.

For a small commission he rolls the pill, furnishes the pipe, and gently rouses the sleeper just as he has reached Rainbow Bend in the Dream-joint.

Brokers are everywhere noted for their Pluck: and all are geese who flock to their roosts.

Brokers are indigenous to all large cities, conspicuous among the several types being those of New York, Boston, Chicago, and Philadelphia.

The New York Broker conducts a kind of modern Trading Post, where Lambs' wool is exchanged for the Skins of Bulls and Bears. His armorial crest shows a pair of sheep shears crossed by a sand-bag, above a shield showing a pump emptying itself upon a bale of stock certificates. His family motto is: "Dare to do Everybody; but do him first!" supplemented by the well-known proverbs, "Rome was not bilked in a day." "The Plunger comes often to Market but goes broke at last."

The Bostonian is a choice survival of the vintage of 1776, who does business according to the rules and regulations of the Society of Mayflower Descendants. To open an account with him you must show a Plymouth Rock pedigree and a Family Tree that's not too shady. His office is kept at cold storage temperature and if you're not in the Blue Book he won't take your money. His specialty is Coppers, which, of course, had an historic record. In 1773, his forefathers held their famous Tea Party disguised as copper-colored savages. Wherefore the Bostonian has clung to Copper ever since. His three Police commissioners are his Trinity Copper, his business cards are printed from copper plate, his fancy still clings to the copper-toed boot, and he's ready to copper a tip from Wall Street as long as he's got the price. His waking and sleeping hours are perpetually controlled by the ancient maxim, "Take care of the Coppers and the Dollars will take care of themselves."

The somnolent gentleman from Philadelphia has little to do in the brokerage business. But, once a year, when the City Street Department mows the pavements, he gets to work to the tune of "Make hay while the sun shines," and occasionally gathers in an Investor with the rest of the tender green blades.

The biography of the Chicago broker makes an interesting cereal story in Wheat, Corn, and Oats, illustrated with drawings from still life of Cattle, Sheep, and Hogs. The trade in wild oats is everywhere brisk, from the Auditorium to Clark Street, though some of the biggest deals are now on the hog. In the Windy City the habit of blowing yourself comes easy, and the Chicago broker, having the manners of a megaphone, does not suffer for lack of self-advertisement.

SPECULATION

Speculating on Margin is an expensive but exciting pastime indulged in by those who find the Shell Game and Three-card Monte too tame for their entertainment.

Speculation is a song and dance specialist which makes the circuit of the principal cities throughout the year. It occupies the Boards of the Bucket-Shop Amusement Company from 10 A.M. TO 3 P.M., daily, Sundays and holidays excepted.

The "turn" includes the repeated rendition, with variations, of a popular melody entitled "When You Ain't Got no Money, why, You Needn' Come Around!" and a clever Buck and Wing performance, in which the artist Bucks the Market while his Margin takes Wings.

For those who care to take part in the performance, we cheerfully submit the following:

THREE GOOD RULES FOR SPECULATING ON MARGIN

1. Don't!
2. Do not!
3. If after careful perusal of the two foregoing Rules, you are still resolved upon Folly, go to your Bank, Cracked Teapot, Old Stocking, or other financial depository where your hard-earned Cash is kept, and having taken therefrom One Thousand Dollars in double eagles, roll them carefully in strong, brown wrapping paper and seal the ends. You are now ready for the next step.

Placing the Roll in your inside vest pocket, proceed briskly to the nearest Ferry slip and take the first boat which leaves. When midway between the termini, walk to the stern of the boat, take the Roll and heave it far out into the troubled waters. Your money will have then arrived at its terminus, and you should calmly proceed to yours.

By following this method of Deposit for your Margin, you not only save Brokers' commissions and Interest but many anxious days and sleepless nights, besides having anticipated by a few hours the inevitable Sinking of your Money.

A STOCK EXCHANGE

A stock exchange is an institution which perpetuates the use of an ancient punitive machine known as Stocks.

Originally Stocks were occupied by the Lawless, entailing great physical suffering; they are now embraced by the Brainless, and the distress is wholly financial.

A Stock Exchange is in fact a Cathedral of Mammon, provided with $20,000 pews and numerous handsomely figured columns.

The edifice has no transepts, but boasts of more than one knave. The worshippers faithfully observe the Order for the Laying on of Hands and expiate the Sins of Commission by frequently offering up a Sacrificial Lamb.

A Stock Exchange is always constructed from Direct Wires and Read Tape, is well posted throughout, and is warranted Bear high and Bull strong.

The two principal Stock Exchanges of America are those of New York and Boston, situated in the streets known as Wall and State. Wherefore, if a man goeth not to the Wall in one city, he may surely attain the impoverished State in the other.

In Stock Exchange Society some of the worst breaks are the result of the best gunning, while no one can accurately estimate the number of probable drops in one small pool.

In accordance with prevailing etiquette, tips circulate freely and are not refused even by the aristocracy.

Foolish Finance - Compiled by Gideon Wurdz
John Luce & Company, Boston, MA: 1904

BIBLIOGRAPHY

A Pleasury of Witticisms and Word Play, Anthony B. Lake. 1965. Bramhall House Publishers, New York, NY 1975

A Treasury of American Folklore, James S. Tidwell. 1956. Crown Publishers, Inc., New York, NY

Can Board Chairmen Get Measles?, Charles Preston. Cartoon Features Syndicate, Cambridge, MA

Cartoons by Martin J. Bucella, Cheektowaga, NY

Cartoons by Dave Carpenter, Emmetsburg, IA

Cartoons by Jack Corbett, Salem, OR

Cartoons by Benita Epstein, Cardiff, CA

Cartoons by James Estes, Amarillo, TX

Cartoons by Oliver Gaspirtz, Brooklyn, NY

Cartoons by John Hayes, Overland Park, KS

Cartoons by Jonny Hawkins, Sherwood, MI

Cartoons by Lo Linkert, Port Coquitlam, B.C. Canada

Cartoons by Luci Meighan, Laytonville, CA

Cartoons by Dan Rosandich, Chassell, MI

Cartoons by Harley Schwadron, Ann Arbor, MI

Cartoons by Andrew Toos, Bridgewater, CT

Cartoons by M.L. Zanco, Waukegan, IL

Early to Bed and Late to Rise, Don Herold. August 1965. Reader's Digest, Reader's Digest Assn., Pleasantville, NY

Foolish Finance, Gideon Wurdz. 1904. John Luce & Co., Publishers. Boston, MA

Humor & Health Journal, J. R. Dunn, Publisher. 1995.

Jackson, MS

John A. Fenn, West Palm Beach, FL

Laughter Prescription Newsletter, Karen Lee, Publisher. Carlsbad, CO

Milton Berle's Comedy Software, Box 3605, Beverly Hills, CA

New Direction Weight Control System, Marcia Proffitt. Wabash County Hospital, Wabash, IN

Nothing Serious...Just a Little Chat With the Boss, Ann E. Weeks, DNS. Passage Publishing, Inc., Louisville, KY

Pepper and Salt (Wall Street Journal), Charles Upton. April 7, 1966. Cartoon Features Syndicate, Cambridge, MA

Pitiless Parodies and Other Outrageous Verses, Frank Jacobs. 1994. Dover Publishing, Mineola, NY

Pun American Newsletter, Lila Bondy. Deerfield, IL

Steve Wilson & Company, Steve Wilson. Bexley, OH

The Best of Snickers, Charles Ghigna. 1994. Southern Publisher's Group. Pelham, AL

The Care and Feeding of Executives and the General Theory of How to Be One, Millard C. Faught and Laurence Hammond. 1945. Wormwood Press, New York, NY

The Mirthful Lyre, Arthur Guiterman. 1918. Harper & Brothers Publishers. New York, NY

Tony Schwartz, 1951. New York, NY

When You're Up to Your Ass in Alligators, Alan Dundes & Carl R. Pagter. Wayne State University Press. Detroit, MI 1987

Work Hard and You Shall Be Rewarded, Alan Dundes & Carl R. Pagter. 1975. Wayne State University Press, Detroit, MI

Write If You Get Work: The Best of Bob & Ray, Bob Elliott & Ray Goulding. 1975. Random House, Inc., New York, NY

Also available from Lincoln-Herndon Press:

*	Grandpa's Rib-Ticklers and Knee-Slappers	$ 8.95
*	Josh Billings–America's Phunniest Phellow	$ 7.95
	Davy Crockett—Legendary Frontier Hero	$ 7.95
	Cowboy Life on the Sidetrack	$ 7.95
	A Treasury of Science Jokes	$ 9.95
	The Great American Liar–Tall Tales	$ 9.95
	The Cowboy Humor of A.H. Lewis	$ 9.95
	The Fat Mascot—22 Funny Baseball Stories and More	$ 7.95
	A Treasury of Farm and Ranch Humor	$10.95
	Mr. Dooley–We Need Him Now! The Irish-American Humorist	$ 8.95
	A Treasury of Military Humor	$10.95
	Here's Charley Weaver, Mamma and Mt. Idy	$ 9.95
	A Treasury of Hunting and Fishing Humor	$10.95
	A Treasury of Senior Humor	$10.95
	A Treasury of Medical Humor	$10.95
	A Treasury of Husband and Wife Humor	$10.95
	A Treasury of Religious Humor	$10.95
	A Treasury of Farm Women's Humor	$12.95
	A Treasury of Office Humor	$10.95
	A Treasury of Cocktail Humor	$10.95

*Available in hardback

The humor in these books will delight you, brighten your conversation, make your life more fun and healthier, because "Laughter is the Best Medicine."

Order From:
Lincoln-Herndon Press, Inc.
818 South Dirksen Parkway
Springfield, IL 62703
(217) 522-2732